ENGLISH FIRST

STARTER

Robert Hickling

Misato Usukura

KINSEIDO

Kinseido Publishing Co., Ltd.
3-21 Kanda Jimbo-cho, Chiyoda-ku,
Tokyo 101-0051, Japan

Copyright © 2014 by Robert Hickling
　　　　　　　　 Misato Usukura

All rights reserved. No part of this publication may be
reproduced, stored in a retrieval system, or
transmitted, in any form or by any means, electronic,
mechanical, photocopying, recording or otherwise,
without the prior permission of the publisher.

First published 2014 by Kinseido Publishing Co., Ltd.

Design: parastyle inc.
Illustrations: Yukiko Yuze

音声ファイル無料ダウンロード　

http://www.kinsei-do.co.jp/download/3969

この教科書で　DL 00 の表示がある箇所の音声は、上記 URL または QR コードにて無料でダウンロードできます。自習用音声としてご活用ください。

▶ PC からのダウンロードをお勧めします。スマートフォンなどでダウンロードされる場合は、
　 ダウンロード前に「解凍アプリ」をインストールしてください。
▶ URL は、**検索ボックスではなくアドレスバー (URL 表覧)** に入力してください。
▶ お使いのネットワーク環境によっては、ダウンロードできない場合があります。

CD 00　左記の表示がある箇所の音声は、教室用 CD（Class Audio CD）に収録されています。

はしがき

English First Starter は中学校・高校で学んだ基本的な文法事項を順序立てて総復習することを目指した教材で、比較的やさしいレベルの単語や構文が使われているため、英語に苦手意識を持っている人であっても無理なく学習を進めることができます。とある日本の大学に通う4人の大学生がこの教科書の主な登場人物です。そのうちの2人は日本人の学生（アキ、ケンジ）で、あとの2人は留学生（アリス、ジャスティン）です。この4人のおもしろおかしい大学生活の物語を題材に、英語を聞いたり、読んだり、話したり、書いたりする活動を通して、英語の力を伸ばします。全15ユニットあり、1ユニットは5ページです。

各ユニットは以下の5つのセクションで構成されています。（　　）内は活動時間の目安です。

Listening Warm Up

A イラストを見ながら短めの英文を聞いて、簡単な問いに答えます。（5〜10分）
B 40語程度の英文を聞いて、True/False の問題に答えます。（5〜10分）

Conversation

A 会話を聞いて空欄に入る語を埋めます。各ユニットでターゲットになっている文法項目を含んだ箇所が空欄になっています。（5〜10分）
B もう一度会話を聞いて、内容に関する質問（選択式）に答えます。（5〜10分）
C ペアになって会話の音読練習をします。（5分）

Grammar Points

各ユニットのターゲット文法項目について、簡単な例文を提示しながら日本語で説明します。また、このセクションの冒頭に基本例文を3つ示していますので、文法に苦手意識を持っている人はまずはこれらを文章ごと覚えましょう。（10分）

Grammar Check

A 選択式の文法練習問題。各ユニットのターゲット文法項目の理解を確実なものにします。（5〜10分）
B 英語の基本語順に慣れるための文法練習問題。日本語の意味に合うように与えられた英単語を並び替えて英文を作ります。（5〜10分）

Express Yourself

🅐 登場人物が自身について語っている40語程度の文章を読みます。後に続く🅑に備えるためのモデル文でもあるので、読んで確認します。（5〜10分）

🅑 ここでは、🅐で読んだ文章を参考にして、自分自身について英語で表現します。どのような内容を盛り込むのか、どのような表現を使うのかについてもヒントが提示されますので、書くことが苦手な人でも取り組めます。（10分）

さらに、巻末には付録として、各章の Grammar Points で紹介した基本例文「まずはこれを覚えよう！」と、不規則変化動詞を一覧にしてまとめています。自習・復習に活用してください。

以上のタスクを通じて、学生の皆さんに英語の楽しさを知ってもらえれば幸いです。

最後に、本書作成にあたり金星堂編集部の皆様から多くのご助言、ご支援をいただきました。この場をお借りして御礼申し上げます。

著者一同

本書は CheckLink（チェックリンク）対応テキストです。

CheckLinkのアイコンが表示されている設問は、CheckLinkに対応しています。
CheckLinkを使用しなくても従来通りの授業ができますが、特色をご理解いただき、授業活性化のためにぜひご活用ください。

CheckLinkの特色について

　大掛かりで複雑な従来のe-learningシステムとは異なり、CheckLinkのシステムは大きな特色として次の3点が挙げられます。

1. これまで行われてきた教科書を使った授業展開に大幅な変化を加えることなく、専門的な知識なしにデジタル学習環境を導入することができる。
2. PC教室やCALL教室といった最新の機器が導入された教室に限定されることなく、普通教室を使用した授業でもデジタル学習環境を導入することができる。
3. 授業中での使用に特化し、教師・学習者双方のモチベーション・集中力をアップさせ、授業自体を活性化することができる。

▶教科書を使用した授業に「デジタル学習環境」を導入できる

　本システムでは、学習者は教科書のCheckLinkのアイコンが表示されている設問にPCやスマートフォン、携帯電話端末からインターネットを通して解答します。そして教師は、授業中にリアルタイムで解答結果を把握し、正解率などに応じて有効な解説を行うことができるようになっています。教科書自体は従来と何ら変わりはありません。解答の手段としてCheckLinkを使用しない場合でも、従来通りの教科書として使用して授業を行うことも、もちろん可能です。

▶教室環境を選ばない

　従来の多機能なe-learning教材のように学習者側の画面に多くの機能を持たせることはせず、「解答する」ことに機能を特化しました。PCだけでなく、一部タブレット端末やスマートフォン、携帯電話端末からの解答も可能です。したがって、PC教室やCALL教室といった大掛かりな教室は必要としません。普通教室でもCheckLinkを用いた授業が可能です。教師はPCだけでなく、一部タブレット端末やスマートフォンからも解答結果の確認をすることができます。

▶授業を活性化するための支援システム

　本システムは予習や復習のツールとしてではなく、授業中に活用されることで真価を発揮する仕組みになっています。CheckLinkというデジタル学習環境を通じ、教師と学習者双方が授業中に解答状況などの様々な情報を共有することで、学習者はやる気を持って解答し、教師は解答状況に応じて効果的な解説を行う、という好循環を生み出します。CheckLinkは、普段の授業をより活力のあるものへと変えていきます。

　上記3つの大きな特色以外にも、掲示板などの授業中に活用できる機能を用意しています。従来通りの教科書としても使用はできますが、ぜひCheckLinkの機能をご理解いただき、普段の授業をより活性化されたものにしていくためにご活用ください。

CheckLink の使い方

CheckLinkは、PCや一部タブレット端末、スマートフォン、携帯電話端末を用いて、この教科書の CheckLink のアイコン表示のある設問に解答するシステムです。
- 初めてCheckLinkを使う場合、以下の要領で**「学習者登録」**と**「教科書登録」**を行います。
- 一度登録を済ませれば、あとは毎回**「ログイン画面」**から入るだけです。CheckLinkを使う教科書が増えたときだけ、改めて**「教科書登録」**を行ってください。

CheckLink URL

https://checklink.kinsei-do.co.jp/student/

QRコードの読み取りができる端末の場合はこちらから ▶▶▶

ご注意ください！ 上記URLは**「検索ボックス」**でなく**「アドレスバー(URL表示欄)」**に入力してください。

▶学習者登録

① 上記URLにアクセスすると、右のページが表示されます。学校名を入力し「ログイン画面へ」をクリックしてください。
PCの場合は「PC用はこちら」をクリックしてPC用ページを表示します。同様に学校名を入力し「ログイン画面へ」をクリックしてください。

② ログイン画面が表示されたら**「初めての方はこちら」**をクリックし「学習者登録画面」に入ります。

③ 自分の学籍番号、氏名、メールアドレスを入力し、次に任意のパスワードを8桁以上20桁未満（半角英数字）で入力します。なお、学籍番号はパスワードとして使用することはできません。

④「パスワード確認」は、❸で入力したパスワードと同じものを入力します。

⑤ 最後に「登録」ボタンをクリックして登録は完了です。次回からは、「ログイン画面」から学籍番号とパスワードを入力してログインしてください。

▶教科書登録

①ログイン後、メニュー画面から「教科書登録」を選び（PCの場合はその後「新規登録」ボタンをクリック）、「教科書登録」画面を開きます。

②教科書と受講する授業を登録します。
教科書の最終ページにある、**教科書固有番号**のシールをはがし、印字された**16桁の数字とアルファベット**を入力します。

③授業を担当される先生から連絡された**11桁の授業ID**を入力します。

④最後に「登録」ボタンをクリックして登録は完了です。

⑤実際に使用する際は「教科書一覧」（PCの場合は「教科書選択画面」）の該当する教科書名をクリックすると、「問題解答」の画面が表示されます。

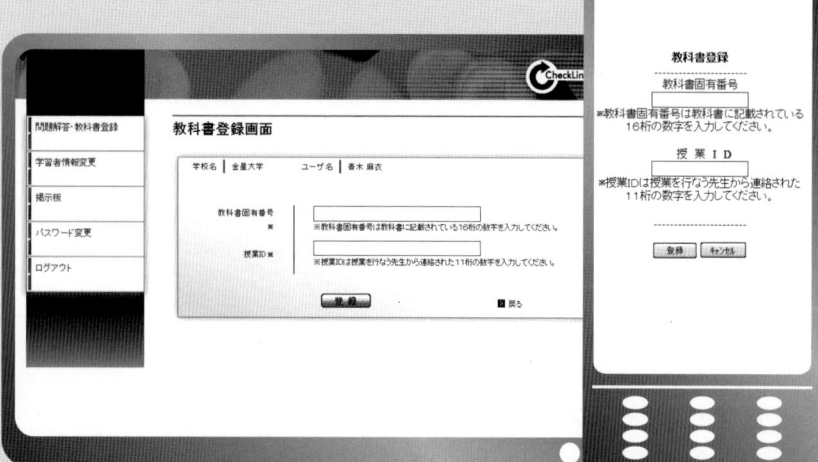

▶問題解答

①問題は教科書を見ながら解答します。この教科書の CheckLink のアイコン表示のある設問に解答できます。

②問題が表示されたら選択肢を選びます。

③表示されている問題に解答した後、「解答」ボタンをクリックすると解答が登録されます。

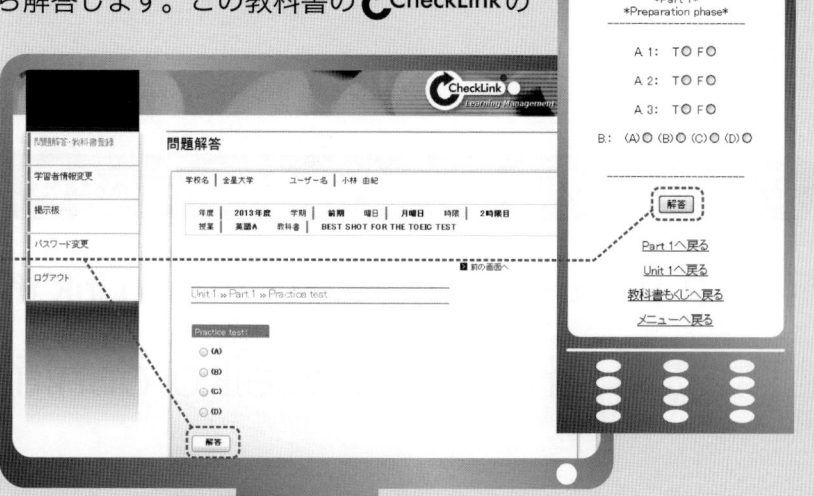

▶CheckLink 推奨環境

PC

推奨 OS
　Windows XP, Vista 以降
　Macintosh OS X 以降
　Linux

推奨ブラウザ
　Internet Explorer 6.0 以上
　Firefox 3.0 以上
　Safari
　Opera
　Google Chrome

携帯電話・スマートフォン

3G 以降の携帯電話（docomo, au, softbank）
iPhone, iPad
Android OS スマートフォン、タブレット

▶CheckLink 開発

CheckLink は奥田裕司 福岡大学教授、正興 IT ソリューション株式会社、株式会社金星堂によって共同開発されました。

CheckLink は株式会社金星堂の登録商標です。

CheckLink の使い方に関するお問い合わせは…

正興 IT ソリューション株式会社　CheckLink 係

e-mail　checklink@seiko-denki.co.jp

Table of Contents

Pre-Unit ——————————————————————————— 10

Unit 1	**It's Nice to Meet You** be 動詞	12
Unit 2	**Take a Hike** 一般動詞	17
Unit 3	**Don't Wear Your High Heels** 代名詞	22
Unit 4	**There's Nothing in My Backpack** 場所を表す前置詞	27
Unit 5	**What a Small World!** Yes・No で答える疑問文	32
Unit 6	**Let's Eat** 現在進行形・過去進行形	37
Unit 7	**It's a Date** 一般動詞の過去形	42
Unit 8	**I Have to Study** 助動詞	47
Unit 9	**What Do You Think of My Sketch?** 疑問詞	52
Unit 10	***Kanji* Is So Difficult** 不定詞・動名詞	57
Unit 11	**I'll Make a Birthday Cake** 未来形	62
Unit 12	**Saturday or Sunday?** 接続詞	67
Unit 13	**I'm Not Good with Computers** 現在完了形	72
Unit 14	**Which Is Better?** 比較級・最上級	77
Unit 15	**Surprise!** 受動態	82

付 録

「基本例文」一覧 ——————————————————————— 88
「不規則変化動詞」一覧 ————————————————————— 91

Pre-Unit

▶ このユニットでは英語の基本語順を勉強します。日本語の語順との違いに注意しましょう。

●英語の基本語順

［例］

誰が （主語）	どうする （動詞）	何を
I	play	soccer.

「私はサッカーをします」

Check!

A　語順に注意しながら（　　）内の語句を並べかえて文を作ってみましょう。

1. 私はコーヒーを飲みます。(drink / I / coffee)

   _____

2. 彼女は中国語を話します。(Chinese / speaks / She)

   _____

B　英文の意味を書きましょう。

1. I practice the piano.

   _____

2. Tom plays basketball.

   _____

●基本語順＋追加情報

[例]

誰が (主語)	どうする (動詞)	何を	追加情報	
I	play	soccer	at school on Sunday.	「私は日曜日に学校でサッカーをします」

A 語順に注意しながら（　）内の語句を並べかえて文を作ってみましょう。

1. 私は毎朝公園でテニスをします。
   (tennis / every morning / play / in the park / I)
   _____

2. 私たちは今日学校で剣道の練習をします。
   (practice / we / today / *kendo* / at school)
   _____

B 英文の意味を書きましょう。

1. I eat lunch with my friends every day.
   _____

2. Lisa takes pictures at a park in the morning.
   _____

11

Unit 1 It's Nice to Meet You
be 動詞

Check Points

❶ この教科書に出てくる登場人物について、基本的な情報を理解しましょう。
❷ 英語で自己紹介できるようになりましょう。
❸ be 動詞を使った英文に慣れましょう。

Listening Warm Up

A 以下のイラストは、この教科書の登場人物に関するものです。イラストを見ながら英文を聞き、内容が正しい場合は T を、間違っている場合は F を○で囲みましょう。

1. (T / F)   2. (T / F)   3. (T / F)

B アリスとジャスティンについて紹介している英文を聞いて、1〜3の内容が正しい場合はTを、間違っている場合はFを○で囲みましょう。

1. Alice and Justin are in Japan to learn Japanese.   (T / F)
2. Alice's hobby is taking pictures.   (T / F)
3. Justin is a shy person.   (T / F)

It's Nice to Meet You   Unit **1**

Conversation

▶ 留学生のアリスが、日本語の授業のクラスメートのジャスティンに話しかけています。

A 会話を聞いて空欄を埋めましょう。 DL 04   CD 04

Alice: Hi. My name (¹   ) Alice.
Justin: Hello. (²   ) Justin.
Alice: (³   ) nice to meet you Justin. (⁴   ) you from the States?
Justin: No, I'm (⁵   ). I'm from Vancouver, Canada.
Alice: Oh, Vancouver. That (⁶   ) far from my home. I'm from Seattle.
Justin: Yeah, that *is* close.
Alice: Hey, let's practice speaking Japanese together sometime. *Ii desu ka?*
Justin: Umm… pardon?

B もう一度会話を聞いて、1〜3の英文について、適切な語を選びましょう。   CheckLink

1. Alice and Justin (**a.** are **b.** aren't) good friends.
2. Justin is from (**a.** Seattle **b.** Vancouver).
3. Vancouver (**a.** is **b.** isn't) far from Seattle.

C クラスメートとペアを組んで、アリスとジャスティンの会話を声に出して練習してみましょう。

Grammar Points

> **まずは これを 覚えよう！**
>
> I am 18 years old.「私は18歳です」
> You are a quiet person.「あなたはおとなしい人です」
> Justin is shy.「ジャスティンは恥ずかしがり屋です」

● 基本語順

　［主語（誰が）］＋［be動詞］＋［どうだ］

● 主語とbe動詞の組み合わせ

	主語（誰が）	be動詞	どうだ	
単数	I	am	18 years old.	「私は18歳です」
単数	You	are	a quiet person.	「あなたはおとなしい人です」
単数	He / She	is	shy.	「彼／彼女は恥ずかしがり屋です」
単数	It	is	in the kitchen.	「それは台所にあります」
複数	We / You / They	are	good friends.	「私たち／あなたたち／彼らは良い友達です」

● be動詞の過去形

	主語（誰が）	be動詞（過去形）	どうだ	
単数	I / He / She / It	was	the captain of the soccer team.	「私／彼／彼女／それ／あなたはサッカー部のキャプテンでした」
単数	You	were		
複数	We / You / They	were	popular in the class.	「私たち／あなたたち／彼らはクラスの人気者でした」

● 否定文

　否定文を作るときはbe動詞の後ろにnotをつけます。

　David is not [isn't] a talkative person.「デービッドはおしゃべりな人ではありません」
　David was not [wasn't] a talkative person.「デービッドはおしゃべりな人ではありませんでした」

Grammar Check

A （　）内のa～cから適当なものを選び、○で囲みましょう。

1. I (**a.** am **b.** are **c.** is) British.

2. Sara (**a.** am **b.** are **c.** is) Australian.

3. The children (**a.** am **b.** are **c.** is) in the bedroom.

4. Don is (**a.** America **b.** from American **c.** from America).

5. Richard (**a.** is Canadian **b.** are from Canada **c.** is Canada).

6. (**a.** Mai and Mari are **b.** Mai and Mari is **c.** Mai and Mari they are) the same age.

7. James (**a.** are **b.** was **c.** were) at home yesterday afternoon.

8. Kate and Sally (**a.** are **b.** was **c.** were) good friends ten years ago.

B （　）内の語句を並べ替えて文を作りましょう。

1. (from / Alice / United States / the / is)　「アリスはアメリカ出身です」

　_____.

2. (teachers / are / Alice and Justin / English / not)
「アリスとジャスティンは英語の先生ではありません」

　_____.

3. (quiet / a / he / is / person)　「彼はおとなしい人です」

　_____.

4. (old / years / am / I / 18)　「私は18歳です」

　_____.

5. (big / a / is / Canada / country)　「カナダは大きい国です」

　_____.

Express Yourself

A アリスが自己紹介しています。英文を読んで内容を理解しましょう。　　DL 05　CD 05

Hello. My name is Alice. I'm American. I'm from Seattle, Washington. I'm 19 years old. I'm a student at Kokusai Koryu University. There are four people in my family—my mother, my father, my older brother and me.

B アリスの自己紹介の英文を参考にして、自分自身を紹介する英文を書いてみましょう。

項目	英文
名前	My name is (¹).
国籍	I'm (²).
出身地	I'm from (³).
年齢	I'm (⁴) years old.
大学名	I'm a student at (⁵).
家族	There are (⁶) people in my family.

Take a Hike

Unit 2

一般動詞

Check Points

❶ ケンジやジャスティンの日々のスケジュールや週末の予定を理解しましょう。
❷ 1日の行動を英語で説明できるようになりましょう。
❸ 一般動詞を使った英文に慣れましょう。

Listening Warm Up

A 1〜3の英文を聞いて、内容が一致するイラストをa〜cから選びましょう。

a

b

c

1. _____　　2. _____　　3. _____

B ケンジは日曜日には何をするのでしょうか。1〜3の内容が正しい場合はTを、間違っている場合はFを○で囲みましょう。

1. Kenji gets up late.　　　　　　　　　　(T / F)
2. He rides his bicycle.　　　　　　　　　 (T / F)
3. He eats breakfast at a restaurant.　　 (T / F)

17

Conversation

▶ ケンジはジャスティンを日曜日の遊びに誘います。

A 会話を聞いて空欄を埋めましょう。

Kenji: Justin, you (¹   ) to take pictures, right?

Justin: Yeah, I (²   ) pictures every day.

Kenji: What kind of pictures?

Justin: Oh, anything—people, buildings, trains. And I often (³   ) to parks and take pictures of flowers and birds.

Kenji: Oh, really? Aki and I sometimes (⁴   ) in the mountains. We're going on Sunday. (⁵   ) with us.

Justin: OK. I (⁶   ) (⁷   ) any plans on Sunday. That (⁸   ) great! Thanks.

Kenji: No problem. (⁹   ) (¹⁰   ) your camera.

Notes • plan「予定」

B もう一度会話を聞いて、1〜3の英文について、適切な語を選びましょう。

1. Justin (**a.** likes **b.** doesn't like) to take pictures of buildings and trains.
2. Kenji and Aki sometimes (**a.** drive **b.** hike) in the mountains.
3. Justin (**a.** has plans **b.** doesn't have any plans) on Sunday.

C クラスメートとペアを組んで、ケンジとジャスティンの会話を声に出して練習してみましょう。

Grammar Points

> **まずはこれを覚えよう!**
>
> Justin likes cameras very much.「ジャスティンはカメラが大好きです」
> Bring your dictionary to class.「授業には辞書を持ってきなさい」
> I don't have any plans today.「私は今日は特に予定はありません」

● 基本語順

主語が I、You 以外の単数形の場合、動詞に s（最後の文字によっては es や ies）をつけます。

主語（誰が）	動詞	何を	その他の情報	
I	like	sushi	very much.	「私は寿司が大好きです」
Justin	likes	cameras	very much.	「ジャスティンはカメラが大好きです」
Aki	studies	English	with Kenji.	「アキはケンジと一緒に英語を勉強します」

● 否定文

否定文を作るときは、動詞の前に don't や doesn't をつけます。主語が I、You、複数形の場合は don't を、I、You 以外の単数形の場合は doesn't を使います。

主語	don't/doesn't＋動詞	何を	その他の情報	
I	don't have	any plans	today.	「今日は特に予定はありません」
Steve	doesn't play	golf.		「スティーブはゴルフをしません」

● 命令文

命令文（「～しなさい」）を作るときは、動詞（原形）から文を始めます。命令文の否定形（「～してはいけません」「～しないで」）を作るときは、動詞の前に Don't を入れます。また、命令文の前に Let's を入れることで「～しようよ」という意味になります。

主語	動詞	何を	その他の情報	
―	Bring	your dictionary	to class.	「授業には辞書を持ってきなさい」
―	Don't bring	your dictionary	to class.	「授業には辞書を持ってきてはいけません」
―	Let's have	a party	for Jane.	「ジェーンのためにパーティーをひらこうよ」

Grammar Check

A （　）に入れるのに最も適当な動詞を1つ選び、1～5については肯定形を、6～10については否定形を書きましょう。空欄に入る語は一語とは限りません。

1. I (　　　　　) a lot of homework this week.
2. Kohei's dad (　　　　　) golf every Sunday.
3. Mr. Kitson (　　　　　) math.
4. Those students (　　　　　) from China.
5. The baby always (　　　　　) when he is hungry.
6. Gary lives in Japan, but he (　　　　　) Japanese.
7. I (　　　　　) to restaurants very often.
8. This train (　　　　　) at every station.
9. Elephants (　　　　　) meat.
10. It (　　　　　) often in London.

come
cry
have
play
teach

eat
go
snow
speak
stop

B （　）内の語句を並べ替えて文を作りましょう。

1. (my / always / homework / do / I)「私はいつも宿題をやります」
   _____.

2. (Paris / in / sister / Eri's / lives)「エリの姉妹はパリに住んでいます」
   _____.

3. (any / don't / have / I / money)「私はお金をまったく持っていません」
   _____.

4. (doesn't / my car / much / use / gas)「私の車は多くのガソリンを使いません」
   _____.

5. (Paris / a postcard / me / send / from)「パリから葉書を送ってください」
   Please _____.

Take a Hike　Unit **2**

Express Yourself

A ジャスティンが1日のスケジュールについて紹介しています。英文を読んで内容を理解しましょう。

DL 09　CD 09

I'd like to talk about my Monday schedule. I get up at 7:00. I leave home at 8:00. At 8:45 I arrive at my university. I go to school by train. I have three classes. My first class starts at 9:00. My last class finishes at 4:30.

B 上の英文を参考にして、1週間のある曜日のスケジュールについて英語で表現してみましょう。

項目	英文
曜日	I'd like to talk about my (^{1}　　　　　) schedule.
起床時間	I (^{2}　　　) up at (^{3}　　　　　).
家を出る時間	I (^{4}　　　　　) home at (^{5}　　　　　).
学校に着く時間	I (^{6}　　　　　) at my university at (^{7}　　　　　).
通学方法	I (^{8}　　　) to school (^{9}　　　) (^{10}　　　　　　).
授業数	I (^{11}　　　　) (^{12}　　　　　　) class/classes.
最初の授業の開始時間	My first class (^{13}　　　　) at (^{14}　　　　).
最後の授業の終了時間	My last class (^{15}　　　　) at (^{16}　　　　).

Hints ［交通手段を表す言葉］
• 「バスで」by bus　• 「徒歩で」on foot　• 「自転車で」by bicycle

21

Unit 3　Don't Wear Your High Heels

代名詞

❶ 登場人物の家族や友達についての情報を理解しましょう。
❷ 自分の家族や親しい友人を英語で紹介できるようになりましょう。
❸ 代名詞を使った英文に慣れましょう。

Listening Warm Up

A 1〜3の英文を聞いて、それぞれが示すイラストをa〜cから選びましょう。

1. _____　　2. _____　　3. _____

B アリスが自分の兄を紹介しています。1〜3の内容が正しい場合はTを、間違っている場合はFを○で囲みましょう。

1. Her brother's name is Jim.　　　　　　　　　(T / F)
2. Her brother likes to play tennis.　　　　　　(T / F)
3. Her brother has a girlfriend named Tammy.　(T / F)

Unit 3 Don't Wear Your High Heels

Conversation

▶ アキがアリスをハイキングに誘っています。何が必要なのでしょうか。

A 会話を聞いて空欄を埋めましょう。　🎧 DL 12　💿 CD 12

Aki: Alice, I'm going hiking in the mountains with Kenji and (¹   ) friend on Sunday. Please come with (²   ).

Alice: All right. Is it far?

Aki: No, (³   ) takes about 50 minutes by train to get there.

Alice: OK. …Oh, (⁴   ) don't have a backpack or hiking boots.

Aki: That's all right. (⁵   ) brother has a backpack. You can use (⁶   ).

Alice: What about hiking boots?

Aki: (⁷   ) don't need hiking boots. Just don't wear (⁸   ) high heels. Ha ha ha!

Notes • backpack「リュックサック」

B もう一度会話を聞いて、1〜3の英文について、適切な語を選びましょう。　CheckLink

1. It takes about (**a.** 15　**b.** 50) minutes to get to the mountains by train.
2. Alice (**a.** has a backpack but no hiking boots　**b.** doesn't have a backpack or hiking boots).
3. Aki tells Alice that she doesn't need (**a.** a backpack　**b.** hiking boots).

C クラスメートとペアを組んで、アリスとアキの会話を声に出して練習してみましょう。

Grammar Points

> **まずは これを 覚えよう!**

This is my brother. His name is John.
「これは私の兄です。彼の名前はジョンです」
I know Mrs. Johnson. I met her yesterday.
「ジョンソンさんなら知っています。私は彼女と昨日会いました」
My mother bakes bread. It is delicious.
「私の母はパンを焼きます。それは美味しいです」

●代名詞の働き

代名詞は前に出てきた名詞を言い換えるときに使います。

Paul and I are good friends. We always have lunch together.
「ポールと僕は仲が良いです。僕たちはいつもお昼を一緒に食べます」

I bought a new pair of shoes. How do you like them?
「新しい靴を買ったんだ。(それらを)どう思う?」

My favorite color is green. What's yours?
「私のお気に入りの色は緑です。あなたの(好きな色)は?」

●代名詞の格変化

代名詞は文中でどのような意味になるかによって形が変化します。

	主格 「〜は／〜が」 主語になる	所有格 「〜の」 後ろには名詞が来る	目的格 「〜を」 目的語になる 前置詞の後に来る	所有代名詞 「〜のもの」
単数	I	my	me	mine
	you	your	you	yours
	he	his	him	his
	she	her	her	hers
	it	its	it	―
複数	we	our	us	ours
	you	your	you	yours
	they	their	them	theirs

Grammar Check

A （　）内のa〜cから適当なものを選び、○で囲みましょう。

1. This is my brother. (**a.** He **b.** Him **c.** His) name is Pete.
2. The concert tickets are expensive. (**a.** It **b.** Its **c.** They) cost ¥10,000.
3. This is Mary's book. Please give it to (**a.** she **b.** her **c.** hers).
4. Hitomi lives with (**a.** her **b.** hers **c.** she) sister.
5. The blue umbrella is (**a.** me **b.** my **c.** mine).
6. I have new glasses. Do you like (**a.** it **b.** them **c.** their)?
7. Brad and (**a.** I **b.** my **c.** mine) like to play sports.
8. Is this Yoko's pen, or is it (**a.** you **b.** your **c.** yours)?
9. Steve meets (**a.** him **b.** his **c.** she) girlfriend every Sunday.
10. My hobby is tennis. What's (**a.** it **b.** its **c.** yours)?

B （　）内の語句を並べ替えて文を作りましょう。

1. (city / a / Canada / it's / in)　「ジャスティンはバンクーバー出身です。それはカナダにある都市です」
Justin is from Vancouver. _____.

2. (textbook / my / have / don't / I)　「どうしよう！ 教科書を持っていないや」
Oh, no! _____.

3. (are / Linda / brother / her / and)　「リンダと彼女の兄弟は学生です」
_____ students.

4. (report / tomorrow/ give / your / me)　「あなたのレポートを明日私に提出してください」
Please _____.

5. (your / mine / this / or / pen)　「これはあなたのペンですか、それとも私のものですか」
Is _____?

Express Yourself

A アキが自分の親友を紹介しています。英文を読んで内容を理解しましょう。

DL 13　CD 13

My best friend's name is Harumi. I met her six years ago at school. She is 19 years old. Her birthday is in April. She's kind and also very funny. She's good at sports. Sometimes we go to a karaoke box.

B 上の英文を参考にして、自分の親友を紹介する英文を書いてみましょう。架空の友人を想定して書いてもかまいません。

項目	英文
親友の名前	My best friend's name is (¹　　　　　　).
知り合った時期と場所	I met (²　　　) (³　　　　　　) years ago at (⁴　　　　　　).
親友の年齢	(⁵　　　) is (⁶　　　　　　) years old.
親友の誕生月	(⁷　　　) birthday is in (⁸　　　　　　).
親友の性格など	(⁹　　　) is (¹⁰　　　　　　) and (¹¹　　　　　　).
親友が得意なこと	(¹²　　　) is good at (¹³　　　　　　).
ときどき親友と一緒にやること	Sometimes we (¹⁴　　　　　　).

Hints
- 「気さく」friendly ・「感じが良い」nice ・「明るい」cheerful
- 「ゲームをする」play games ・「ショッピングをする」go shopping
- 「カフェで紅茶／コーヒーを飲む」have tea/coffee at a café

There's Nothing in My Backpack

Unit 4

場所を表す前置詞

Check Points

❶ アリスとアキが準備しているハイキングに関する情報を理解しましょう。
❷ 自分の身の回りにあるものの位置関係を英語で説明できるようになりましょう。
❸ 前置詞を使った英文に慣れましょう。

Listening Warm Up

A 1〜3のイラストについて英文が読まれます。内容と一致するものはTを、一致しないものはFを○で囲みましょう。

CheckLink　DL 14　CD 14

1. (T / F)　　2. (T / F)　　3. (T / F)

B ジャスティンは姉が住んでいるアパートについて話しています。1〜3の内容が正しい場合はTを、間違っている場合はFを○で囲みましょう。

CheckLink　DL 15　CD 15

1. Grace lives in Chicago. 　　　　　　　　　(T / F)
2. Grace's apartment is on the fifth floor. 　(T / F)
3. Grace doesn't like her apartment. 　　　(T / F)

Conversation

▶ アリスとアキは山へ行こうと準備をしているところです。

A 会話を聞いて空欄を埋めましょう。　　　DL 16　　CD 16

Aki: Are you ready for our hike, Alice?

Alice: Umm, no. There's nothing (¹　　　) my backpack.

Aki: OK, there's some mineral water (²　　　) the kitchen table. And there's a map (³　　　) (⁴　　　) the newspaper.

Alice: …I don't see the map.

Aki: Then look (⁵　　　) the newspaper. Is it there?

Alice: …Yeah. Got it. Do I need a towel?

Aki: Yes, there's one (⁶　　　) my backpack. I put a hat and sunglasses (⁷　　　) it for you, too.

Alice: Thanks. What about food?

Aki: Let's make some rice balls for everyone.

B もう一度会話を聞いて、1〜3の英文について、適切な語を選びましょう。　　CheckLink

1. There's some water (**a.** in the kitchen　**b.** on the coffee table).
2. The map is (**a.** next to　**b.** under) the newspaper.
3. The hat and sunglasses are (**a.** in Aki's backpack　**b.** on the towel).

C クラスメートとペアを組んで、アキとアリスの会話を声に出して練習してみましょう。

Unit 4 There's Nothing in My Backpack

Grammar Points

まずはこれを覚えよう！

There's nothing in my backpack.
「私のリュックサックの中には何も入っていません」
I put a hat and sunglasses on the backpack.
「私は帽子とサングラスをリュックサックの上に置きました」
Your shoes are under the table.「あなたの靴はテーブルの下です」

●前置詞の働き

「～の中に」とか「～の上に」というように場所を表したいときには前置詞を使います。前置詞の後ろに「机」などの場所を表す言葉が続きます。

●前置詞の種類

前置詞	例文
at 「～で」	I often eat lunch at a café. 「私はよくカフェでお昼を食べます」
in 「～の中に・で」	My mother often does yoga in the living room. 「私の母はよく居間でヨガをします」
on 「～の上に・で」	Don't touch anything on the desk. 「机の上のものには手を触れるな」
above 「～の上の方に・で」	The balloon went up above the clouds and disappeared. 「その風船は雲の上へと昇り、そして消えた」
under 「～の下に・で」	Your shoes are under the table. 「あなたの靴はテーブルの下です」
around 「～の周りに・で」	Mrs. Smith always wears a beautiful scarf around her neck. 「スミス先生はいつも首の周りにきれいなスカーフをしている」
behind 「～の後ろに・で」	A big building stands behind our house. 「私たちの家の後ろに大きなビルが建っています」
between 「～の間に・で」	Kent always sits between Maria and me. 「ケントはいつもマリアと私の間に座る」
in front of 「～の前に・で」	The red car in front of my house is my uncle's. 「家の前の赤い車は叔父さんのものです」
next to 「～の隣に・で」	The seat next to me is empty. 「私の隣の席は空いています」

Grammar Check

A ( )内のa～cから適当なものを選び、○で囲みましょう。

1. Minoru is not here now. He's (**a.** at **b.** in **c.** on) work.

2. Haruka is (**a.** at **b.** in **c.** on) her room.

3. Your keys are (**a.** above **b.** in **c.** on) the table.

4. There's a bus stop (**a.** above **b.** between **c.** in front of) the library.

5. Linda always wears a chain (**a.** around **b.** at **c.** between) her neck.

6. There's a restaurant (**a.** between **b.** next to **c.** to) the bank.

7. The subway runs (**a.** above **b.** on **c.** under) the city.

8. In the alphabet, Q comes (**a.** behind **b.** between **c.** in front of) P and R.

9. Look up. There are some birds flying (**a.** above **b.** on **c.** under) us.

10. Look straight ahead. Don't look (**a.** at **b.** behind **c.** in front of) you.

B ( )内の語句を並べ替えて文を作りましょう。

1. (station / meet / the / let's / at) 「駅で会いましょう」
   _____.

2. (Takuya / me / sits / to / next) 「タクヤは教室で私の隣に座っています」
   _____ in class.

3. (alien / house / in / an / the) 「なんてことだ！家の中に異星人がいる」
   Oh no! There's _____.

4. (the / sleeps / bed / under / the dog) 「その犬はベッドの下で眠ります」
   _____.

5. (yellow / behind / line / stand / the) 「黄色い線の内側にお立ちください」
   Please _____.

Express Yourself

A ケンジが自分の机の上やまわりにあるものについて紹介しています。英文を読んで内容を理解しましょう。

Let me tell you where some things are on my desk. My computer monitor is on the desk in the center. There's a printer next to it. An alarm clock is behind the mouse pad. My keyboard is in front of my monitor. My computer mouse is on the mouse pad beside the keyboard.

Notes ・Let me tell you...「〜を紹介します」

B 上の英文を参考にして、下の絵の中にあるアイテムの場所を説明する英文を書いてみましょう。場所を表す前置詞を4種類以上使ってみましょう。

アイテム	英文
辞書	My dictionary is (¹) the desk.
カレンダー	There's a calendar (²) the dictionary.
スマートフォン	My smartphone is (³) the calendar.
テニスラケット	My tennis racket is (⁴) the door.
ノート型PC	My laptop computer is (⁵) the table (⁶) the center.

Unit 5 What a Small World!

Yes・Noで答える疑問文

Check Points

❶ アリスたちのハイキング当日の様子を理解しましょう。
❷ 相手に英語で質問をして、必要な情報を聞き出せるようになりましょう。
❸ 英語の疑問文の使い方に慣れましょう。

Listening Warm Up

A 1〜3の英文が読まれます。a〜cのどの吹き出しに入るのが適切か答えましょう。

CheckLink　DL 18　CD 18

1. _____　2. _____　3. _____

B アリスがハイキングについてメールで質問し、アキが答えています。1〜3の内容が正しい場合はTを、間違っている場合はFを○で囲みましょう。

CheckLink　DL 19　CD 19

1. The mountain is high.　　　　　　　　　　(T / F)
2. It's not cold at the top of the mountain.　(T / F)
3. Kenji's friend is American.　　　　　　　　(T / F)

Conversation

▶ 今日はみんなでハイキングです。ケンジの友達のカナダ人とは？

A 会話を聞いて空欄を埋めましょう。　　🎧 DL 20　💿 CD 20

Aki: Alice, (¹　　　) you (²　　　) Kenji?
Alice: No, I don't. …Wait. There he is.
Kenji: …Hi, Aki. Hi, Alice. (³　　　) (⁴　　　) late?
Alice: Hi, Kenji. No, you're not late. (⁵　　　) (⁶　　　) alone?
Kenji: No, my friend is in the washroom. …Oh, here he comes.
Alice: …Hi, Justin.
Justin: Alice! Hi.
Aki: Alice, (⁷　　　) you (⁸　　　) Justin?
Alice: Yes. We're in the same Japanese class. What a small world!

Notes ・What a small world!「世の中せまいわね！」

B もう一度会話を聞いて、1〜3の英文について、適切な語を選びましょう。　　⟳ CheckLink

1. Aki and Alice meet (**a.** Justin　**b.** Kenji) first.
2. Kenji (**a.** is　**b.** isn't) late.
3. Justin (**a.** is　**b.** isn't) surprised to see Alice.

C クラスメートと組んで、4人の会話を声に出して練習してみましょう。

Grammar Points

> **まずはこれを覚えよう！**
>
> Is Juliet from Hawaii?「ジュリエットはハワイ出身ですか」
> Do you speak Spanish?「あなたはスペイン語を話しますか」
> Does your brother play the violin?
> 「あなたのお兄さんはバイオリンを弾きますか」

● Be 動詞の疑問文

主語と be 動詞の位置を入れ替えて、疑問文を作ります。

肯定文	疑問文と応答文
You are a soccer fan.	Are you a soccer fan? 「あなたはサッカーファンですか」 → Yes, I am. / No, I'm not.
Juliet is from Hawaii.	Is Juliet from Hawaii? 「ジュリエットはハワイ出身ですか」 → Yes, she is. / No, she isn't.
Maya and Saki are twins.	Are Maya and Saki twins? 「マヤとサキは双子ですか」 → Yes, they are. / No, they aren't.

● 一般動詞の疑問文

文頭に Do あるいは Does を置いて、疑問文を作ります。主語が I や You 以外の単数の場合は Does を、それ以外の場合は Do を使います。動詞の形は常に原形です。

肯定文	疑問文と応答文
You speak Spanish.	Do you speak Spanish? 「あなたはスペイン語を話しますか」 → Yes, I do. / No, I don't.
Your brother plays the violin.	Does your brother play the violin? 「あなたのお兄さんはバイオリンを弾きますか」 → Yes, he does. / No, he doesn't.

Grammar Check

A （　）内のa〜cから適当なものを選び、○で囲みましょう。

1. (**a.** Are **b.** Do **c.** Is) you cold?
2. (**a.** Are **b.** Do **c.** Does) you like your English class?
3. (**a.** Do **b.** Does **c.** Is) your brother have a girlfriend?
4. (**a.** Do **b.** Does **c.** Is) their car new?
5. (**a.** Are **b.** Do **c.** Is) your hobby dancing?
6. (**a.** Does **b.** Is **c.** Do) this train go to Tokyo Station?
7. (**a.** Are **b.** Do **c.** Does) you speak Chinese?
8. (**a.** Are **b.** Do **c.** Does) Tim and Meg friends?
9. (**a.** Do **b.** Does **c.** Are) we need a ticket?
10. (**a.** Are **b.** Does **c.** Is) there any fruit in the basket?

B 例を参考にしてYes/Noで答えられる質問文を作りましょう。

例▶ They like sushi. → Do they like sushi?

1. Justin is Canadian. → _____?
2. Alice likes parties. → _____?
3. Aki and Kenji speak English well.

   → _____?

4. Kenji and Aki are good friends.

   → _____?

5. Justin has a nice camera.

   → _____?

Express Yourself

A ジャスティンは日本の人から色々な質問をされるそうです。英文を読んで内容を理解しましょう。

DL 21　CD 21

Here are three questions that Japanese people often ask me. Number 1: Are you American? Number 2: Do you like Japan? Number 3: Are you an English teacher?

These are my answers. Number 1: No, I'm not American. I'm Canadian. Number 2: Yes, I love Japan. The people and the food are great! Number 3: No, I'm not an English teacher. I'm a student. I study Japanese.

B あなたがインタビューしたいと思う相手を決めて、その人に聞いてみたいと思う質問を3つ考えてみましょう。インタビューの相手はあなたにとって身近な人でも良いですし、有名人やスポーツ選手、歴史上の人物でもかまいません。質問文の書き出しは Are you...? か Do you...? を使いましょう。書き終わったら、その答えを書きましょう。

インタビューしたい相手	
Q1	
A1	
Q2	
A2	
Q3	
A3	

Hints
- 出身地をたずねる　Are you from（場所）?
- 職業をたずねる　Are you（職業）?
- 好きなもの・人をたずねる　Do you like...?
- 得意なことをたずねる　Are you good at...?
- 性格をたずねる　Are you a（性格を表す言葉）person?
  [性格を表す言葉]
  「親切な」kind ／「まじめな」serious ／「明るい」cheerful ／「力強い」powerful

Let's Eat

Unit 6

現在進行形・過去進行形

Check Points

❶ ハイキングでどのようなことが起こっているのか理解しましょう。
❷ 自分が今やっていることを英語で説明できるようになりましょう。
❸ 現在進行形・過去進行形を使った英文に慣れましょう。

Listening Warm Up

A 1〜3のイラストについて英文が読まれます。内容と一致するものはTを、一致しないものはFを○で囲みましょう。

CheckLink　DL 22　CD 22

1
2
3

1. (T / F)　2. (T / F)　3. (T / F)

B ハイキング中のケンジの心の中を覗いてみましょう。1〜3の内容が正しい場合はTを、間違っている場合はFを○で囲みましょう。

CheckLink　DL 23　CD 23

1. Kenji thinks everyone is having a good time.　(T / F)
2. Justin is laughing a lot.　(T / F)
3. Kenji is asking Alice many questions.　(T / F)

37

Conversation

▶ 食事の時間になりましたが、アキとジャスティンが見当たらないようです。

A 会話を聞いて空欄を埋めましょう。　　　DL 24　CD 24

Alice: Let's eat. Kenji, do you know where Aki and Justin are?
Kenji: They're over there. Justin (¹　　　) (²　　　　　) some pictures, and Aki (³　　　) (⁴　　　　　) a sketch.
Alice: Well, I'm really hungry. (⁵　　　) not (⁶　　　　).
Kenji: It's OK. (⁷　　　　) (⁸　　　　　) back now.
Alice: Oh, good. Aki! Justin! Hurry up! The rice balls (⁹　　　　) (¹⁰　　　　　) cold.
Aki, Justin and Kenji: …Huh?
Alice: Ha ha ha! (¹¹　　　　) just (¹²　　　　　). Come on, let's eat.

B もう一度会話を聞いて、1〜3の英文について、適切な語を選びましょう。　CheckLink

1. Kenji (**a.** knows **b.** doesn't know) where Aki and Justin are.
2. Alice is (**a.** a little **b.** very) hungry.
3. Alice tells her friends (**a.** a joke **b.** a story).

C クラスメートと組んで、4人の会話を声に出して練習してみましょう。

Let's Eat　Unit **6**

Grammar Points

まずはこれを覚えよう!

I am making breakfast now.「私は今、朝食を作っています」
Ken was playing basketball with his friends then.
「ケンはその時、友達とバスケットボールをしていました」
Your sister is not singing on stage now.
「あなたのお姉さんは今ステージで歌っていません」

●基本語順

主語	be動詞	一般動詞 ing形	何を	その他の情報	
I	am	making	breakfast	now.	「私は今、朝食を作っています」

●現在進行形・過去進行形

現在進行形では現在形のbe動詞を、過去進行形では過去形のbe動詞を使います。

現在進行形	過去進行形
I am making breakfast now. 「私は今、朝食を作っています」	I was making breakfast then. 「私はその時、朝食を作っていました」
Ken is playing basketball with his friends now. 「ケンは今、友達とバスケットボールをしています」	Ken was playing basketball with his friends then. 「ケンはその時、友達とバスケットボールをしていました」
The girls are drawing pictures now. 「少女たちは今、絵を描いています」	The girls were drawing pictures then. 「少女たちはその時、絵を描いていました」

●否定文と疑問文

否定文を作るときはbe動詞の後ろにnotを入れます。
疑問文を作るときは「主語」と「be動詞」の位置を入れ替えます。

	Your sister is singing on stage now.	「あなたのお姉さんは今ステージで歌っています」
否定文	Your sister is not singing on stage now.	「あなたのお姉さんは今ステージで歌っていません」
疑問文	Is your sister singing on stage now?	「あなたのお姉さんは今ステージで歌っていますか」

Grammar Check

A (　　)内のa〜cから適当なものを選び、○で囲みましょう。

1. This party is fun. I (**a.** have **b.** do have **c.** am having) a good time.
2. Nozomi and Risa (**a.** are **b.** do **c.** is) shopping right now.
3. Slow down! (**a.** You **b.** Your **c.** You're) driving too fast.
4. Ken isn't working. (**a.** He golfs **b.** He's golfing **c.** He does golf).
5. (**a.** Are the kids sleep **b.** The kids sleeping **c.** Are the kids sleeping) now?
6. Please don't talk now. (**a.** I'm **b.** I'm not **c.** I wasn't) studying.
7. It (**a.** is rain **b.** is raining **c.** was raining) hard last night.
8. (**a.** Are you wearing **b.** Do you wearing **c.** You wearing) contact lenses?
9. (**a.** Are **b.** Was **c.** Were) you watching TV at 10:00 last night?
10. We (**a.** aren't **b.** wasn't **c.** weren't) listening, so the teacher got angry.

B (　　)内の語句を並べ替えて文を作りましょう。

1. (you / for / Koji / waiting / is)　「コウジはあなたを待っていますよ」
   _____.

2. (watching / you / movie / a / are)　「映画を見ているのですか」
   _____?

3. (everybody / me / to / is / listening)　「みなさん私の言うことを聞いていますか」
   _____?

4. (well / working / computer / wasn't / my)
   「私のコンピューターは昨日うまく動いていませんでした」
   _____ yesterday.

5. (report / writing / you / your / were)　「あなたは昨晩レポートを書いていたのですか」
   _____ last night?

Express Yourself

A アキがハイキングの時の写真を眺めています。英文を読んで内容を理解しましょう。

DL 25　CD 25

I'm looking at three photographs of my hike with Alice, Kenji and Justin yesterday. In the first photo, Justin is eating *natto* for the first time. There's *natto* all over his face. In the second photo, Kenji is using a knife and fork to eat his rice ball. It's so funny! In the third photo, Kenji and Justin are carrying Alice up the mountain. She was so tired!

B 下記の3つの場面にいる自分自身を想像してみましょう。そして、あなたがそこで何をしているのかを説明する英文を、現在進行形を使って書いてみましょう。

| 場面1 | あなたは大学の図書館にいます。何をしていますか。 |

I'm in the school library.
I'm (¹　　　　　　　　　　　　　　　　　　　　　　　).

| 場面2 | あなたは大学の最寄駅にいます。何をしていますか。 |

I'm at the closest station to my university.
I'm (²　　　　　　　　　　　　　　　　　　　　　　　).

| 場面3 | あなたは家族と一緒に家にいます。何をしていますか。 |

I'm with my family at home.
I'm / We're (³　　　　　　　　　　　　　　　　　　　).

Hints
- 「宿題をやる」doing homework
- 「調べ物をする」doing research
- 「レポートを書く」writing a report
- 「友人を待つ」waiting for my friend
- 「電車の切符を買う」buying a train ticket
- 「夕飯を食べる」having dinner
- 「テレビを観る」watching TV

Unit 7 It's a Date

一般動詞の過去形

Check Points

❶ みんながハイキングでどのような思い出を作ったのか、情報を理解しましょう。
❷ その日自分がしたことを英語で説明できるようになりましょう。
❸ 過去形を使った英文に慣れましょう。

Listening Warm Up

A 1〜3のイラストについて英文が読まれます。内容と一致するものはTを、一致しないものはFを○で囲みましょう。

CheckLink　DL 26　CD 26

1.（T / F）　2.（T / F）　3.（T / F）

B ジャスティンとアリスが受けた漢字テストの結果を英文で聞いて、1〜3の内容が正しい場合はTを、間違っている場合はFを○で囲みましょう。

CheckLink　DL 27　CD 27

1. Justin got 100% on his *kanji* test.　（T / F）
2. Justin studied for the test.　（T / F）
3. Alice studied a lot for the test.　（T / F）

Conversation

▶ ジャスティンはアキの趣味に興味があるようです。

A 会話を聞いて空欄を埋めましょう。　　DL 28　CD 28

Aki: (¹　　　) you (²　　　) the hike on Sunday, Justin? You (³　　　) a lot of pictures.

Justin: I (⁴　　　) a great time. And you (⁵　　　) many sketches.

Aki: Do you want to see them? I (⁶　　　) them with me.

Justin: Sure. …Wow, these are really good, Aki.

Aki: Do you sketch, Justin?

Justin: Me? No. I (⁷　　　) sketching once, but the trees (⁸　　　) (⁹　　　) like trees.

Aki: Well, do you want me to give you a few sketching lessons?

Justin: Yes. Thanks. How about next Sunday?

Aki: It's a date.

B もう一度会話を聞いて、1〜3の英文について、適切な語や文を選びましょう。　CheckLink

1. (**a.** Justin showed Aki his photos　**b.** Aki showed Justin her sketches).
2. Justin tried sketching (**a.** once　**b.** many times).
3. Aki and Justin made plans for (**a.** next Saturday　**b.** next Sunday).

C クラスメートとペアを組んで、アキとジャスティンの会話を声に出して練習をしてみましょう。

Grammar Points

まずはこれを覚えよう!

I practiced *kendo* yesterday. 「私は昨日剣道の練習をしました」
Alice didn't study for the math test.
「アリスは数学のテスト勉強をしなかった」
Did Lisa and Bob find a nice apartment?
「リサとボブは良いアパートを見つけましたか」

●一般動詞の過去形

動詞の過去形には、規則変化(動詞の原形に[e]dをつける)するものと、不規則変化をするものがあります。不規則変化する動詞はGrammar CheckのAと巻末の「不規則変化動詞」一覧で覚えましょう。

主語(誰が)	動詞の過去形	何を	その他の情報	
I	practiced ↑ (practice)	*kendo*	yesterday.	「私は昨日剣道の練習をしました」
Kate and Jessica	brought ↑ (bring)	sandwiches	to the picnic.	「ケイトとジェシカはピクニックにサンドイッチを持っていきました」

●否定文と疑問文

否定文を作るときは「主語」の後にdidn'tを入れ、動詞は原形に直します。
疑問文を作る時は「主語」の前にDidを入れ、動詞は原形に直します。

	Lisa and Bob found a nice apartment.	「リサとボブは良いアパートを見つけました」
否定文	Lisa and Bob didn't find a nice apartment.	「リサとボブは良いアパートを見つけませんでした」
疑問文	Did Lisa and Bob find a nice apartment?	「リサとボブは良いアパートを見つけましたか」

Grammar Check

A 以下の動詞を、過去形にしましょう。

1. be (was/were)
2. have (　　　)
3. say (　　　)
4. do (　　　)
5. write (　　　)
6. make (　　　)
7. see (　　　)
8. go (　　　)
9. come (　　　)
10. know (　　　)
11. find (　　　)
12. take (　　　)
13. get (　　　)
14. give (　　　)
15. think (　　　)
16. tell (　　　)
17. put (　　　)
18. read (　　　)

B 以下の(　)に入る単語を枠内から選び、過去形にして文を完成させましょう。

1. Aki, Alice, Justin and Kenji (　　　) hiking yesterday.
2. Aki and Alice (　　　) rice balls for everyone.
3. The weather (　　　) good—sunny and warm.
4. They (　　　) some rabbits and other small animals.
5. Everyone (　　　) lots of water.

> be
> drink
> go
> make
> see

C (　)内の語句を並べ替えて文を作りましょう。

1. (interesting / I / an / read / book)「私は先週おもしろい本を読みました」
   _____ last week.

2. (find / textbook / your / you / did)「あなたは教科書を見つけましたか」
   _____?

3. (his / Mike / didn't / homework / finish)「マイクは宿題を終わらせませんでした」
   _____.

4. (a / work / Laura / took / taxi/ to)「ローラはタクシーで仕事に行きました」
   _____.

Express Yourself

A アリスが今朝したことを話しています。英文を読んで内容を理解しましょう。

DL 29　CD 29

This morning I got up at 7:30. First I checked my email. Then I put on my clothes. After that I ate breakfast. I had *miso* soup and rice and a cup of green tea. Then I brushed my teeth, brushed my hair and put on my make-up. Then I put my books in my bag and went to school.

B 上の英文を参考にして、あなたが今朝起きてからやったことを、順番に5つ英語で書いてみましょう。

項目	英文
起床時間	This morning I (¹　　　　　　) up at (²　　　　　　).
朝起きて最初にやったこと	First I (³　　　　　　　　　　　　　　　).
次にやったこと3つ	Then I (⁴　　　　　　　　　　　　), (⁵　　　　　　　　　　　　), and (⁶　　　　　　　　　　　　).
さらにやったこと1つ	After that I (⁷　　　　　　　　　　　　).

Hints
- 「友達にメールを書いた」wrote an email to my friend
- 「SNSサイトにコメントした」posted a comment on SNS

I Have to Study

Unit 8

助動詞

Check Points

❶ アリスができないこと、やらなければならないことは何か理解しましょう。
❷ 自分ができること、やらなければならないことを言えるようになりましょう。
❸ 助動詞を使った英文に慣れましょう。

Listening Warm Up

A 1〜3の英文を聞いて、内容が一致するイラストをa〜cから選びましょう。

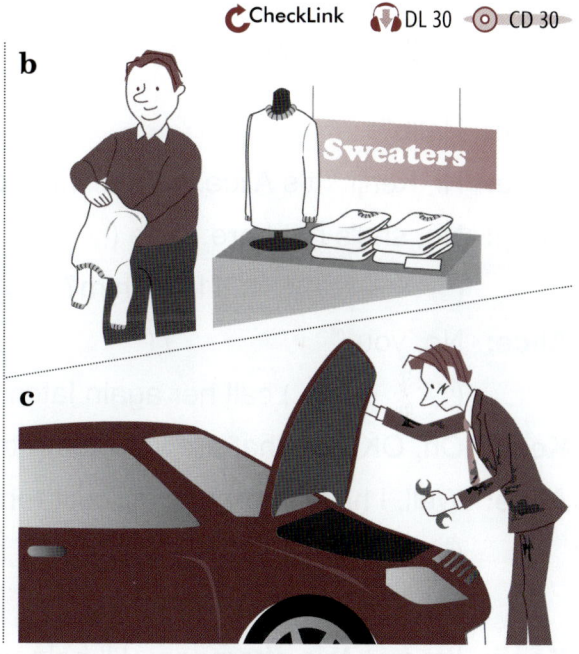

CheckLink　DL 30　CD 30

a

b

c

1. _____　2. _____　3. _____

B 今日のアキの予定をみてみましょう。1〜3の内容が正しい場合はTを、間違っている場合はFを○で囲みましょう。

CheckLink　DL 31　CD 31

1. Aki has classes in the morning.　　　　　　(T / F)
2. She will meet Justin at 1:00.　　　　　　　(T / F)
3. She has to buy some new colored pencils.　(T / F)

47

Conversation

▶ アリスは漢字の勉強をしていますが、困っています。

A 会話を聞いて空欄を埋めましょう。　　　　　DL 32　CD 32

Kenji: Hello?

Alice: Hi, Kenji. It's Alice. Is Aki with you? I (¹　　　　) contact her.

Kenji: No, she's not here. She (²　　　　) be with Justin. (³　　　　　　) I call him?

Alice: No, you (⁴　　　　) (⁵　　　　) (⁶　　　　) do that. I (⁷　　　　) call her again later.

Kenji: Oh, OK. …What are you doing today, Alice?

Alice: Well, I have another *kanji* test tomorrow, so I (⁸　　　　) (⁹　　　　) study. That's why I called Aki. I thought maybe she (¹⁰　　　　) help me.

Kenji: I'm free this afternoon. I'll help you.

B もう一度会話を聞いて、1〜3の英文について、適切な語を選びましょう。　　CheckLink

1. Alice (**a.** can **b.** can't) contact Aki.
2. (**a.** Kenji **b.** Alice) thinks that Aki and Justin might be together.
3. Alice's *kanji* test is (**a.** this afternoon **b.** tomorrow).

C クラスメートとペアを組んで、ケンジとアリスの会話を声に出して練習してみましょう。

I Have to Study Unit **8**

Grammar Points

まずは これを 覚えよう！
I can speak Japanese and English.「私は日本語と英語が話せます」
I must give this book to Mai.「私はこの本をマイに渡さなければならない」
Should I bring my lunch with me?「私はお昼ご飯を持っていくべきですか」

● 助動詞の基本語順

［誰が（主語）］＋［助動詞］＋［～する（動詞原形）］＋［何を］

● 助動詞の種類

助動詞	例文
can 「～できる」「～してもよい」	I can speak Japanese and English. 「私は日本語と英語が話せます」
could 「～できた」	I thought Bob could speak Spanish. 「私はボブがスペイン語を話せると思っていました」
should 「～すべき」	You should go to the doctor right now. 「あなたは今すぐに医者に行くべきだ」
must 「～しなければならない」	I must give this book to Mai. 「私はこの本をマイに渡さなければならない」
have to / has to 「～しなければならない」	The boys have to wear uniforms at school. 「その少年たちは学校で制服を着なければならない」
don't have to / doesn't have to 「～する必要はない」	The boys don't have to wear uniforms at school. 「その少年たちは学校で制服を着なくてもよい」
might 「～かもしれない」	You might be surprised to hear his news. 「君は彼のニュースを聞いて驚くかもしれないよ」

● 否定文と疑問文

否定文を作るときは助動詞の後ろにnotをつけます。
疑問文を作るときは主語と助動詞の順番を入れ換えます。

	I should bring my lunch with me.	「私はお昼ご飯を持っていくべきです」
否定文	I should not bring my lunch with me.	「私はお昼ご飯を持っていくべきではありません」
疑問文	Should I bring my lunch with me?	「私はお昼ご飯を持っていくべきですか」

Grammar Check

A （　　）内のa〜cから適当なものを選び、○で囲みましょう。　　↻CheckLink

1. She (**a.** cans　**b.** can　**c.** can to) sing very well.

2. Timmy is afraid of water. He (**a.** can't swim　**b.** can't to swim　**c.** can't swimming).

3. He (**a.** doesn't have to　**b.** doesn't has to　**c.** don't have to) work today.

4. (**a.** Are we can　**b.** We can　**c.** Can we) take pictures in this museum?

5. We should (**a.** careful　**b.** to careful　**c.** be careful).

6. Take your umbrella. It (**a.** couldn't　**b.** has to　**c.** might) rain tonight.

7. I'm tired. I (**a.** couldn't　**b.** might not　**c.** don't have to) go to the barbecue.

8. Kate (**a.** have to　**b.** having to　**c.** must) be at the airport at 8:00 a.m.

9. You (**a.** don't have to　**b.** might not　**c.** shouldn't) talk in the library.

10. I (**a.** couldn't　**b.** might not　**c.** shouldn't) finish my report last night.

B （　　）内の語句を並べ替えて文を作りましょう。

1. (see / you / we / not / might)　「私たちは明日あなたに会わないかもしれません」
   _____tomorrow.

2. (here / shouldn't / pictures / take / you)　「あなたはここで写真をとるべきではありません」
   _____.

3. (well / English / can / speak / Eri)　「エリは英語を上手く話せますか」
   _____?

4. (work / to / I / have / don't)　「すごくうれしい！今日は仕事をする必要がないんです」
   I'm so happy! _____ today.

5. (I / your / party / go / couldn't / to)　「あなたのパーティーに行かれなくてすみませんでした」
   I'm sorry _____.

Express Yourself

A ケンジが自分の大学について説明しています。英文を読んで内容を理解しましょう。

🎧 DL 33 ◉ CD 33

At my university, we can't drive to school, but we can ride bicycles. There is no parking for cars, motorcycles, or scooters. We don't have to go to all of our classes, but we have to attend 70% of them. We should not be late for class. On rainy or snowy days, we should leave home a little early.

B 上の英文を参考にして、あなたが通っていた中学校あるいは高校の校則について、(　　)内の助動詞を使って英文にしましょう。

校則	英文
やってはいけないこと（can't）	Students (^{1}　　　　　　　　　).
やらなければならないこと（have to）	Students (^{2}　　　　　　　　　).
やる必要がないこと（don't have to）	Students (^{3}　　　　　　　　　).
やってもよいこと（can）	Students (^{4}　　　　　　　　　).

Hints
- 「髪を染める」dye their hair
- 「携帯を持ってくる」bring their cellphones
- 「制服を着る」wear a uniform
- 「自転車で通学する」ride their bicycle to school
- 「お弁当を持ってくる」bring a *bento*

Unit 9 What Do You Think of My Sketch?

疑問詞

Check Points
❶ 絵の描き方について、ジャスティンがアキに質問する内容を理解しましょう。
❷ 場所や価格について英語で質問できるようになりましょう。
❸ 疑問詞を使った疑問文の使い方に慣れましょう。

Listening Warm Up

A 1〜3の英文が読まれます。a〜cのどの吹き出しに入るのが適切か答えましょう。

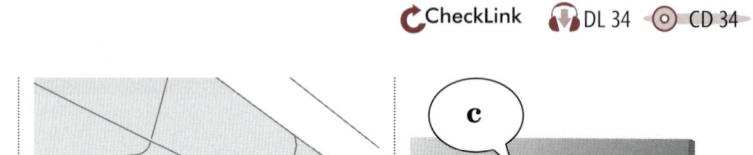

CheckLink　DL 34　CD 34

1. _____　2. _____　3. _____

B ジャスティンの趣味に関する英文を聞いて、1〜3の内容が正しい場合はTを、間違っている場合はFを◯で囲みましょう。

CheckLink　DL 35　CD 35

1. Justin's father works for a fashion magazine.　　（ T / F ）
2. Justin loved going places with his father to take pictures.　（ T / F ）
3. Justin got his first camera when he was five years old.　（ T / F ）

Unit 9 What Do You Think of My Sketch?

Conversation

▶ 今日は日曜日です。アキとジャスティンは公園に絵を描きにきました。

A 会話を聞いて空欄を埋めましょう。　　　　　　　　　　DL 36　CD 36

Justin: This is a nice park. (¹　　　　) do you want to sit?

Aki: Here. We can sketch the pond, the trees and the flowers.

Justin: OK. (²　　　　) do I start my sketch?

Aki: Start with the outline of the pond. Then you can draw the trees and flowers.

Justin: (³　　　　) do I add the colors?

Aki: You can do that later.

Justin: …Well, (⁴　　　　) do you think of my sketch, Aki?

Aki: It's good, Justin. But (⁵　　　　) is there a rabbit in the pond?

Justin: It's not a rabbit. It's a duck.

Aki: Ha ha ha! I know. Just kidding.

Notes ・pond「池」 ・just kidding「冗談だよ」

B もう一度会話を聞いて、1〜3の英文について、適切な語を選びましょう。　CheckLink

1. Aki tells Justin to sketch the (**a.** pond　**b.** trees and flowers) first.
2. Aki thinks Justin's sketch is (**a.** funny　**b.** good).
3. Justin sketched (**a.** a duck in the pond　**b.** a rabbit next to the pond).

C クラスメートとペアを組んで、ジャスティンとアキの会話を声に出して練習してみましょう。

53

Grammar Points

> **まずは これを 覚えよう！**
>
> What do you have in your pocket?「あなたはポケットの中に何を持っていますか」
> Where do you want to go?「あなたはどこへ行きたいのですか」
> How do you say this in English?「あなたはこれを英語でどう言いますか」

● 疑問詞の種類

what	何	who	誰	where	どこ
when	いつ	why	なぜ	how	どのように

● 疑問文の作り方

たずねたい情報（＝疑問詞）は文頭に来ます。

疑問詞（＋名詞／形容詞）	疑問文（[do/does/did＋主語＋動詞]／[be動詞＋主語]）
What 何を	do you have in your pocket? あなたはポケットの中に持っていますか。
What sport 何の（スポーツを）	do you like? あなたは好きですか。
Who 誰を	do you like best in this group? このグループの中であなたは一番好きですか。
Who 誰が	sent the flowers? 花を送りましたか。 ※「誰が〜ですか」という意味の疑問文は、Whoの直後にすぐ動詞が来ます。
Where どこに	do you want to go this weekend? あなたは今週末行きたいですか。
When いつ	did Dan and Maria get married? ダンとマリアは結婚しましたか。
Why なぜ	was Jim late for the test? ジムは試験に遅れたのですか。
How どのように	do you say this in English? あなたはこれを英語で言いますか。
How tall どのくらい（背が高い）	is your brother? あなたのお兄さんは？

54

Grammar Check

A (　)内のa〜cから適当なものを選び、○で囲みましょう。

1. What (**a.** are your name **b.** is your name **c.** your name is)?
2. Where (**a.** Aki went **b.** went Aki **c.** did Aki go)?
3. What (**a.** university do you go to **b.** do you go to university **c.** is your go to university)?
4. How (**a.** I get **b.** do get I **c.** do I get) to the station from here?
5. Who (**a.** does that man **b.** is that man **c.** that man is) over there?
6. When (**a.** started the movie **b.** did start the movie **c.** did the movie start)?
7. Why (**a.** are you late **b.** you are late **c.** you late)?
8. Where (**a.** Kenji lives **b.** is Kenji lives **c.** does Kenji live)?
9. What (**a.** did you **b.** did you do **c.** you did) on Sunday?
10. How much (**a.** is this computer **b.** this computer **c.** this computer is)?

B Aの下線部が答えになるようにQの疑問文を作りましょう。

1. **Q:** Where _____?
   A: I work at Cuppa Coffee. 「私はクッパカフェで働いています」

2. **Q:** What _____?
   A: My English teacher's name is Mr. Peterson.
   「私の英語の先生の名前はピーターソン先生です」

3. **Q:** When _____?
   A: I went to Hawaii last spring. 「私は昨年の春にハワイに行きました」

4. **Q:** Who _____?
   A: Donna washed the dishes. 「ドナは食器を洗いました」

5. **Q:** How _____?
   A: Jim is 188 cm tall. 「ジムは身長188センチです」

Express Yourself

A アキがジャスティンとの夕食について書いています。英文を読んで内容を理解しましょう。

DL 37　CD 37

I had dinner at an Italian restaurant today. I went with Justin. The restaurant is near Hana Station. I had salad, a small pizza and iced tea. It cost ¥1,000.

B 上の英文を参考にして、あなたが最近外食したお店について、質問に答える形で英語で説明してみましょう。外食をしていない人は行きたかったお店を想定して書いてみましょう。

項目	英文
料理のジャンル いつ行ったか	I had (lunch / dinner) at (a / an) (¹　　　　　　　　) restaurant (²　　　　　　　　).
誰と行ったか (□に✓しよう)	☐ I went with (³　　　　　　　　). ☐ I went alone.
レストランの場所 (最寄駅など)	The restaurant is near (⁴　　　　　　　　).
食べたもの	I ate (⁵　　　　　　　　).
いくら払ったか	It cost (⁶　　　　　　　　) yen.

Kanji Is So Difficult

Unit 10

不定詞・動名詞

Check Points

❶ 漢字の勉強法について、ケンジがアリスに与えている助言を理解しましょう。
❷ 自分が好きなことや嫌いなことについて英語で説明できるようになりましょう。
❸ 不定詞と動名詞を使った英文に慣れましょう。

Listening Warm Up

A 1～3のイラストについて英文が読まれます。内容と一致するものはTを、一致しないものはFを○で囲みましょう。

CheckLink　DL 38　CD 38

1. (T / F)　2. (T / F)　3. (T / F)

B ケンジのアルバイトに関する英文を聞いて、1～3の内容が正しい場合はTを、間違っている場合はFを○で囲みましょう。

CheckLink　DL 39　CD 39

1. Kenji is good at *kanji*. 　(T / F)
2. Kenji began teaching *kanji* to children last month. 　(T / F)
3. Kenji's lessons are difficult for the students to understand. 　(T / F)

Conversation

▶ 勉強で頭を使ったらお腹が空きました。ケンジとアリスは何を食べるのでしょう。

A 会話を聞いて空欄を埋めましょう。　　　DL 40　CD 40

Alice: I (^{1}　　　　) studying *kanji*, but *kanji* is so difficult.
Kenji: Don't worry, Alice. Just (^{2}　　　　) writing them many times. And remember, you (^{3}　　　　) to study every day.
Alice: Right. Thanks for helping me today, Kenji. You're a great teacher.
Kenji: No problem. I (^{4}　　　　) teaching you. Hey, let's get something to eat.
Alice: OK. Where do you (^{5}　　　　) to go?
Kenji: How about going to a sushi shop? You like sushi, don't you?
Alice: I love it! And I (^{6}　　　　) to watch the sushi chefs making it, too.

Notes ・sushi chef「寿司職人」

B もう一度会話を聞いて、1〜3の英文について、適切な語や文を選びましょう。　CheckLink

1. Alice (**a.** likes　**b.** doesn't like) to study *kanji*.
2. (**a.** Alice tells Kenji he's a great teacher　**b.** Kenji tells Alice she's a great student).
3. Alice and Kenji decide to go to (**a.** a bar　**b.** a sushi restaurant).

C クラスメートとペアを組んで、アリスとケンジの会話を声に出して練習してみましょう。

Grammar Points

> **まずは これを 覚えよう！**

You need to finish this report tonight.
「今夜このレポートを仕上げる必要があります」
Ms. Butler enjoys teaching English in Japan.
「バトラーさんは日本で英語を教えることを楽しんでいます」
Alice practices writing *kanji* every day.
「アリスは毎日漢字を書く練習をします」

● 不定詞・動名詞の働き

［何を］の部分に「～すること」というような動作を表す言葉が来るときは、不定詞（to +動詞の原形）か、動名詞（-ing 形）を使います。

● 基本語順

主語（誰が）	一般動詞	何を（不定詞／動名詞）	その他の情報	
My brother	loves	to watch / watching	soccer games on TV.	「私の弟はテレビでサッカーの試合を見るのが大好きです」

● 後ろに不定詞が来る動詞

want, need, decide, hope, learn など

Alice <u>wants</u> to study *kanji*.「アリスは漢字を勉強したいと思っています」
You <u>need</u> to finish this report tonight.「今夜このレポートを仕上げる必要があります」

● 後ろに動名詞が来る動詞

enjoy, mind, finish, practice など

Did you <u>finish</u> eating breakfast?「あなたは朝食を食べ終えましたか」
Ms. Butler <u>enjoys</u> teaching English in Japan.
「バトラーさんは日本で英語を教えることを楽しんでいます」

● どちらが来ても良い動詞

love, like, hate, begin, start など

My brother <u>loves</u> to watch / watching soccer games on TV.
「私の弟はテレビでサッカーの試合を見るのが大好きです」

Grammar Check

A （　　）内のa〜cから適当なものを選び、○で囲みましょう。　　CheckLink

1. Alice and Aki like (**a.** shopping　**b.** to shop　**c.** どちらでもよい).
2. The team needs (**a.** practicing　**b.** to practice　**c.** どちらでもよい) more.
3. Kenji enjoys (**a.** camping　**b.** to camp　**c.** どちらでもよい).
4. Olga began (**a.** taking　**b.** to take　**c.** どちらでもよい) ballet lessons.
5. I have to finish (**a.** writing　**b.** to write　**c.** どちらでもよい) my report today.
6. Mai is learning (**a.** playing　**b.** to play　**c.** どちらでもよい) the piano.
7. Harry hates (**a.** getting up　**b.** to get up　**c.** どちらでもよい) early.
8. Azusa wants (**a.** being　**b.** to be　**c.** どちらでもよい) a dancer.
9. Look! It started (**a.** snowing　**b.** to snow　**c.** どちらでもよい).
10. Kazuko and Rumi practice (**a.** speaking　**b.** to speak　**c.** どちらでもよい) English together every day.

B （　　）内の語句を並べ替えて文を作りましょう。

1. (to / enjoy / I / music / listening)　「私は音楽を聴くことを楽しみます」
   _____.

2. (walk / is / Karen's baby / learning / to)　「カレンの赤ちゃんは歩くことを学んでいます」
   _____.

3. (video games / loves / to / Kenta / play)　「ケンタはビデオゲームをすることが大好きです」
   _____.

4. (you / to / tennis / do / want / play)　「あなたはテニスをやりたいですか」
   _____?

5. (the newspaper / finish / you / did / reading)　「あなたは新聞を読み終わりましたか」
   _____?

Kanji Is So Difficult | Unit **10**

Express Yourself

A アリスが自分の好きなこと、嫌いなことについて話しています。英文を読んで内容を理解しましょう。

DL 41　CD 41

Let me tell you about some of my likes and dislikes. I love to sing (but I'm not very good). I like to go shopping. I like to meet friends. I also enjoy studying Japanese. I don't like doing housework such as washing dishes and washing clothes. And I hate getting up early in the morning!

Notes　・such as...「〜のような」

B 上の英文を参考にして、あなたが好きなこと、嫌いなことについて不定詞か動名詞を使って書いてみましょう。

項目	英文
あなたが大好きなこと (love ＋ to 不定詞／動名詞)	I love (^{1}　　　　　).
あなたが好きなこと (like ＋ to 不定詞／動名詞)	I like (^{2}　　　　　).
あなたが楽しんでやること (enjoy ＋動名詞)	I enjoy (^{3}　　　　　).
あなたがあまり好きではないこと (don't like ＋ to 不定詞／動名詞)	I don't like (^{4}　　　　　).
あなたが大嫌いなこと (hate ＋ to 不定詞／動名詞)	I hate (^{5}　　　　　).

61

Unit 11　I'll Make a Birthday Cake
未来形

> **Check Points**
> ❶ ジャスティンの誕生日のために、みんなが企画している内容を理解しましょう。
> ❷ これからの予定について英語で説明できるようになりましょう。
> ❸ will や be going to を使った英文に慣れましょう。

Listening Warm Up

A 1～3のイラストについて英文が読まれます。空欄の吹き出しに入る英文としてふさわしいものには○を、ふさわしくないものには×をそれぞれ入れましょう。

CheckLink　DL 42　CD 42

1. _____　2. _____　3. _____

B アリスとジャスティンの日本語スピーチについて、1～3の内容が正しい場合はTを、間違っている場合はFを○で囲みましょう。

CheckLink　DL 43　CD 43

1. Alice and Justin are going to make speeches next month.　(T / F)
2. Alice is going to make a speech about Japanese food.　(T / F)
3. Justin is going to talk about Japanese anime.　(T / F)

Unit 11 — I'll Make a Birthday Cake

Conversation

アキとアリスはジャスティンのバースデーパーティーを計画します。

A 会話を聞いて空欄を埋めましょう。 DL 44 CD 44

Aki: I'm (¹   ) to have a party next Saturday, Alice. My parents (²   ) be home, and they said it's OK.

Alice: Great! What kind of party?

Aki: It's a birthday party for Justin. He will (³   ) 21.

Alice: (⁴   ) there be a lot of people there?

Aki: Not a lot—maybe eight. I'm going (⁵   ) order pizza.

Alice: OK. And (⁶   ) make a birthday cake.

Aki: Oh, thanks, Alice. …Oh, and promise not to tell Justin about the party. It's a surprise birthday party.

Alice: OK, I won't (⁷   ) anything.

Notes ・have a party「パーティーを開く」

B もう一度会話を聞いて、1〜3の英文について、適切な語を選びましょう。 CheckLink

1. (a. Aki b. Alice) is going to have a birthday party for Justin next Saturday.
2. Justin will be (a. 20 b. 21) years old on his birthday.
3. Alice (a. is going to b. isn't going to) tell Justin about the party.

C クラスメートとペアを組んで、アキとアリスの会話を声に出して練習してみましょう。

Grammar Points

> **まずはこれを覚えよう！**
>
> I'm going to buy a smartphone.「私はスマートフォンを買う予定です」
> I will carry your suitcase.「あなたのスーツケースを持ってあげましょう」
> Our coach won't come to the game today.「監督は今日、試合に来ません」

●未来形の働き

予定や未来の出来事について表現するときはbe going toとwillを使います。

●be going toの基本語順

主語（誰が）	be動詞＋going to	動詞の原形	何を・その他の情報	
I	am going to	buy	a smartphone.	「私はスマートフォンを買う予定です」
My brother	is going to	graduate	from college next month.	「私の弟は来月大学を卒業します」

●willの基本語順

主語（誰が）	will	動詞の原形	何を・その他の情報	
I	will	carry	your suitcase.	「あなたのスーツケースを持ってあげましょう」
Our coach	will	come	to the game today.	「監督は今日、試合に来ます」

●否定文と疑問文

否定文を作るときは、be動詞またはwillの後ろにnotをつけます。will notは通常は短縮形won'tを使います。

疑問文を作るときは、主語とbe動詞またはwillの位置を入れ替えます。

	be going to	will
否定文	My brother isn't going to graduate from college next month. 「私の弟は来月大学を卒業しません」	Our coach won't come to the game today. 「監督は今日、試合に来ません」
疑問文	Is your brother going to graduate from college next month? 「あなたの弟は来月大学を卒業しますか」	Will our coach come to the game today? 「監督は今日、試合に来ますか」

I'll Make a Birthday Cake | Unit **11**

Grammar Check

A ( ) 内のa～cから適当なものを選び、○で囲みましょう。　CheckLink

1. **A:** What (**a.** are going **b.** you are going **c.** are you going) to wear to the party?
   B: (**a.** I going **b.** I'm going **c.** I'm go) to wear a *kimono*.

2. **A:** (**a.** I'll go to **b.** I'm going to go **c.** I'll going) shopping now.
   B: Wait! (**a.** I'll go **b.** I will to go **c.** I'm going to) with you.

3. **A:** Look! That man (**a.** will to **b.** going to **c.** is going to) fall into the river.
   B: (**a.** I'll call **b.** I'll calling **c.** I'm going to calling) for help.

4. **A:** (**a.** I won't home **b.** I'm won't be home **c.** I won't be home) until 8:00 tonight.
   B: All right. (**a.** I won't making **b.** I'll make **c.** I'm going make) dinner.

5. **A:** Don't tell Kate that (**a.** I'm going to **b.** I'll going **c.** I will to) sell my car.
   B: OK. (**a.** I will **b.** I won't **c.** I'm going to).

B ( ) 内の語句を並べ替えて文を作りましょう。

1. (a new guitar / Nick / going / to buy / is)　「ニックは新しいギターを買う予定です」
   _____.

2. (on / the moon / people / live / will)　「いつの日か人類は月に住むことになるだろうと思います」
   I think _____ one day.

3. (go / to / not / we're / going)　「無料のチケットがありますが、私たちはその試合には行きません」
   We have free tickets, but _____ to the game.

4. (it / you / I'll / for / carry)　「あなたのスーツケースは重そうですね。私が持ってあげましょう」
   Your suitcase looks heavy. _____.

5. (you / home / will / for dinner / be)　「今晩は家で夕食を食べますか」
   _____ tonight?

65

Express Yourself

A ジャスティンが明日の予定について話しています。英文を読んで内容を理解しましょう。

DL 45　CD 45

Tomorrow I'm going to get up at 7:00. In the morning, I'm going to have two classes. I'm going to eat lunch in the university cafeteria. In the afternoon, I'm going to have two classes. At night, I'm going to listen to music and study. I'm going to go to bed at around 12:00.

B 上の英文を参考にして、あなたの明日の予定について、英語で書いてみましょう。

項目	英文
起床時間	I'm going to (¹　　　　　　　　) up at (²　　　　　　　　).
午前中にやること	In the morning, I'm going to (³　　　　　　　　).
お昼を食べる場所	I'm going to eat lunch (⁴　　　　　　　　).
午後にやること	In the afternoon, I'm going to (⁵　　　　　　　　).
夜にやること	At night, I'm going to (⁶　　　　　　　　).
就寝時間	I'm going to go to bed at around (⁷　　　　　　　　).

Hints
- 「カラオケをする」sing karaoke　・「本を読む」read a book　・「甘いものを食べる」eat sweets
- 「ビデオゲームをする」play video games　・「スポーツをする」play sports
- 「友達と話す」chat with my friends　・「友達にメールを送る」email my friend(s)
- 「天気予報をチェックする」check the weather forecast
- 「宿題を終える」finish my homework

Saturday or Sunday?

Unit 12

接続詞

Check Points

❶ ジャスティンの誕生日パーティーについて、詳しい情報を理解しましょう。
❷ おすすめのお店について詳しく英語で説明できるようになりましょう。
❸ 接続詞を使った英文に慣れましょう。

Listening Warm Up

A 1〜3のイラストについて英文が読まれます。内容と一致するものはTを、一致しないものはFを○で囲みましょう。

CheckLink　DL 46　CD 46

1　　　　**2**　　　　**3**

1. (T / F)　　2. (T / F)　　3. (T / F)

B アキのアルバイトに関する英文を聞いて、1〜3の内容が正しい場合はTを、間違っている場合はFを○で囲みましょう。

CheckLink　DL 47　CD 47

1. Aki works as a waiter.　　　　　　　　　(T / F)
2. She works every night from 7 to 11.　　(T / F)
3. The restaurant is not far from her house.　(T / F)

Conversation

▶ アキはケンジに話しかけています。ジャスティンのお祝いのことでしょうか。

A 会話を聞いて空欄を埋めましょう。　　　　　　　　DL 48　CD 48

Aki: Kenji, don't forget about Justin's surprise birthday party this weekend.

Kenji: Oh, yeah. Is it on Saturday (¹　　　　) Sunday?

Aki: Kenji!

Kenji: Just kidding. I know it's on Saturday, (²　　　　) I forgot the time.

Aki: Everyone promised to come at 6:00, (³　　　　) you (⁴　　　　) Justin should come at 6:30.

Kenji: OK. Should I bring some drinks (⁵　　　　) snacks?

Aki: We have drinks, (⁶　　　　) could you bring some potato chips (⁷　　　　) some rice crackers?

Kenji: OK, sure. See you then.

Notes ・rice crackers「せんべい」

B もう一度会話を聞いて、1〜3の英文について、適切な語を選びましょう。　　CheckLink

1. Kenji (**a.** forgot　**b.** didn't forget) what day Justin's birthday party was on.
2. Kenji and Justin will go to Aki's house at (**a.** 6:00　**b.** 6:30) on Saturday.
3. Kenji is going to bring some potato chips (**a.** and　**b.** or) rice crackers.

C クラスメートとペアを組んで、2人の会話を声に出して練習してみましょう。

Grammar Points

まずはこれを覚えよう!

John works on Saturdays and plays golf on Sundays.
「ジョンは土曜日に働き、そして日曜日にゴルフをします」
Ted is smart but lazy. 「テッドは頭はいいけれど怠け者です」
Shall we go out for dinner, or do you want to eat at home?
「外食しますか、それとも家で食べたいですか」

●接続詞の働き
2つ以上の語句や文をつなげるとき、接続詞を使います。

●接続詞の種類

接続詞	例文
and 「〜と」 「そして」	My uncle likes golf and billiards. 「私の叔父はゴルフとビリヤードが好きです」 John works on Saturdays and plays golf on Sundays. 「ジョンは土曜日に働き、そして日曜日にゴルフをします」
but 「しかし」	Ted is smart but lazy. 「テッドは頭はいいけれど怠け者です」 Sally went to see a doctor, but the hospital was closed. 「サリーは医者に行きましたが、病院は閉まっていました」
or 「あるいは」	I want to play tennis or badminton. 「私はテニスかバドミントンをしたいです」 Shall we go out for dinner, or do you want to eat at home? 「外食しますか、それとも家で食べたいですか」
so 「だから」	I want to get a driver's license, so I will go to driving school. 「私は運転免許を取得したいので、教習所に通うつもりです」

Grammar Check

A （　　）内にそれぞれ適当なものを選び、書き入れましょう。

> and　but　or　so

1. Last night I stayed home (　　　　) watched television.
2. We can go to a Japanese restaurant (　　　　) a French restaurant.
3. Steve wanted to talk with Cathy, (　　　　) he was too shy.
4. Kaori left her umbrella on the train, (　　　　) she bought a new one.
5. Tony had dinner, took a bath, watched TV (　　　　) went to bed.
6. I'm busy, (　　　　) please don't talk to me now.
7. Do you want to play tennis, (　　　　) are you too tired?
8. I really want to take a trip, (　　　　) I don't have any money.
9. Kenta was sick, (　　　　) he couldn't go to the party.
10. Helen has a car, (　　　　) she never drives it.

B （　　）内の語句を並べ替えて文を作りましょう。

1. (very / breakfast / she's / so / hungry)
   「マミは朝食を食べなかったので、とてもお腹がすいています」
   Mami didn't have ＿＿＿＿＿＿＿＿＿＿, ＿＿＿＿＿＿＿＿＿＿＿＿＿＿＿＿.

2. (you / I / should / or / wait)　「一緒に行ってほしいですか、それともここで待っているべきですか」
   Do you want me to go with ＿＿＿＿, ＿＿＿＿＿＿＿＿＿＿＿＿ here?

3. (and / Osaka / in / lives / married)　「ミチコの姉は結婚して大阪に住んでいます」
   Michiko's sister is ＿＿＿＿＿＿＿＿＿＿＿＿＿＿＿＿＿＿.

4. (cry / sad / didn't / he / but)　「ジミーはとても悲しかったけれど、泣きませんでした」
   Jimmy was very ＿＿＿＿, ＿＿＿＿＿＿＿＿＿＿＿＿＿＿＿＿.

Saturday or Sunday? Unit 12

Express Yourself

A ケンジが自分のお気に入りのお店について話しています。英文を読んで内容を理解しましょう。

DL 49　CD 49

My favorite fast-food restaurant is My Burger. I like their hamburgers and French fries. The food is very good, but the service is a little slow. I go there three or four times a month.

B 上の英文を参考にして、あなたのお気に入りのファストフード店について英語で書いてみましょう。

項目	英文
店の名前	My favorite fast-food restaurant is (¹　　　　　　).
好きなメニューを2つ	I like their (²　　　　　　) and (³　　　　　　).
好きなところを1つと、あまり好きではないところを1つ	(⁴　　　　　　), but (⁵　　　　　　).
どのくらいの頻度で行くか	I go there (⁶　　　　　　).

Hints
- 「いつも店が混雑している」The restaurant is always crowded.
- 「建物が古い」The restaurant is in an old building.
- 「駐車場がある」The restaurant has a parking lot.
- 「禁煙席がある」The restaurant has a non-smoking area.
- 「お店の雰囲気が良い」The atmosphere in the restaurant is good.
- 「料理の値段が安い」The food is cheap.

［頻度を表すことば］
- 「1回」once　・「2回」twice　・「3回」three times
- 「週に1〜2回くらい」once or twice a week
- 「毎日」every day　・「2日に1回」once every two days

Unit 13 I'm Not Good with Computers

現在完了形

Check Points
❶ ケンジがどのようにジャスティンをパーティーに誘ったかを理解しましょう。
❷ 自分がすでにやり終えたことについて英語で説明できるようになりましょう。
❸ 現在完了を使った英文に慣れましょう。

Listening Warm Up

A 1〜3のイラストについて英文が読まれます。内容と一致するものはTを、一致しないものはFを○で囲みましょう。

CheckLink　DL 50　CD 50

1. (T / F)　2. (T / F)　3. (T / F)

B ジャスティンが日本のマンガについて語っています。1〜3の内容が正しい場合はTを、間違っている場合はFを○で囲みましょう。

CheckLink　DL 51　CD 51

1. Justin likes to make manga illustrations.　(T / F)
2. His favorite Japanese manga is *Dragon Ball*.　(T / F)
3. Reading manga has helped him to learn Japanese.　(T / F)

Conversation

▶ ケンジはジャスティンをアキの家まで連れていかなくてはなりません。でも、パーティーのことは秘密です。

A 会話を聞いて空欄を埋めましょう。　　　DL 52　CD 52

Kenji: (¹　　　) you (²　　　　) any plans for Saturday night?
Justin: Well, I think I'll go to the new Johnny Depp movie.
Kenji: Oh, no! I mean, (³　　　) you (⁴　　　　　) your ticket yet?
Justin: No, I'm going to buy it at the movie theater. Do you want to go?
Kenji: Um, yes. But how about going on Sunday?
Justin: Yeah, OK. …Kenji, are you all right?
Kenji: Yeah. Um, Aki's computer (⁵　　　　) (⁶　　　　　) working. She wants me to look at it on Saturday night. Can you help me?
Justin: Um, yeah, OK.
Kenji: Great!!! I mean, good. Thanks.

B もう一度会話を聞いて、1～3の英文について、適切な語を選びましょう。　CheckLink

1. Justin (**a.** has made **b.** hasn't made) plans for Saturday night.
2. Justin (**a.** has bought **b.** hasn't bought) his movie ticket yet.
3. Justin thinks he is going to Aki's house to (**a.** watch a movie **b.** fix her computer).

C クラスメートとペアを組んで、ケンジとジャスティンの会話を声に出して練習してみましょう。

73

Grammar Points

> **まずはこれを覚えよう！**
>
> I have been to Australia.「私はオーストラリアに行ったことがあります」
> I haven't seen her for a long time.
> 「ずいぶん長いこと彼女には会っていません」
> Have you finished your homework?「宿題はやり終えましたか」

●基本語順

動詞の過去分詞形は、動詞の原形に(e)dをつけるものと、不規則変化をするものがあります。不規則変化する動詞は Grammar Check の **A** や巻末の「不規則変化動詞」一覧で覚えましょう。

主語（誰が）	have/has＋動詞の過去分詞	何を・その他の情報	
I	have visited	Paris once.	「私はパリを一度訪れたことがあります」

●現在完了の意味

意味	例文
経験 「～したことがあります」	I have been to Australia. 「私はオーストラリアに行ったことがあります」 I have seen this movie three times. 「私はこの映画を3回見たことがあります」
継続 「ずっと～しています」	My grandmother has lived in Spain for 50 years. 「私の祖母はスペインに50年間住んでいます」
完了 「～し終わっています」 「～してしまいました」	I have finished my homework. 「私は宿題をやり終えました」 Bob has gone to New York. 「ボブはニューヨークに行ってしまいました」

●否定文と疑問文

否定文を作るときはhaveの後ろにnotを入れます。疑問文を作るときは主語とhaveの位置を入れ替えます。否定文も疑問文も、動詞は過去分詞形のままです。

	I have finished my homework.	「私は宿題をやり終えました」
否定文	I haven't finished my homework.	「私はまだ宿題をやり終えていません」
疑問文	Have you finished your homework?	「あなたは宿題をやり終えましたか」

Grammar Check

A 以下の動詞を過去分詞形にしましょう。

1. be (been)
2. have (　　　)
3. say (　　　)
4. do (　　　)
5. write (　　　)
6. make (　　　)
7. see (　　　)
8. go (　　　)
9. come (　　　)
10. know (　　　)
11. find (　　　)
12. take (　　　)
13. get (　　　)
14. give (　　　)
15. think (　　　)
16. tell (　　　)
17. put (　　　)
18. read (　　　)

B (　　) 内のa〜cから適当なものを選び、○で囲みましょう。

1. Sara (**a.** is **b.** was **c.** has) been to Japan three times.
2. The children (**a.** has gone **b.** have gone **c.** have went) to the park.
3. Oh, no! (**a.** I'm lost **b.** I have lose **c.** I've lost) my money.
4. Brian (**a.** has **b.** have **c.** has had) a cold for a week.
5. Mari (**a.** has been **b.** has ever been **c.** was been) to Canada.

C (　　) 内の語句を並べ替えて文を作りましょう。

1. (many / lived / places / have / in)　「ジュリーとマークはいろいろな場所に住んだことがあります」
   Julie and Mark _____.

2. (seen / times / that movie / you / have)　「あなたはその映画を何回見ましたか」
   How many _____?

3. (for / it / a / rained / hasn't)　「もうずいぶん長いこと雨が降っていません」
   _____ long time.

4. (you / to / been / Korea / have)　「あなたは韓国に行ったことがありますか」
   _____?

Express Yourself

A アキが今日したこと、していないことを考えています。英文を読んで内容を理解しましょう。

DL 53 CD 53

It's 11 o'clock in the morning. I have eaten breakfast. I have had two cups of coffee. I have emailed three friends. I haven't had lunch. I haven't read the newspaper. I haven't watched TV.

B 上の英文を参考にして、あなたが今日やったことと、まだやっていないことについて、英語で質問に答えましょう。

例▶ 質問：朝食は食べましたか？
　　答え：食べた場合　　　　　Yes, I have eaten breakfast.
　　　　　まだ食べていない場合　No, I haven't eaten breakfast yet.

1. 質問：友達にメールを送りましたか。

　　答え：＿＿＿＿＿＿＿＿＿＿＿＿＿＿＿＿＿＿＿＿＿＿＿＿＿＿＿＿＿＿＿＿．

2. 質問：昼食は食べましたか。

　　答え：＿＿＿＿＿＿＿＿＿＿＿＿＿＿＿＿＿＿＿＿＿＿＿＿＿＿＿＿＿＿＿＿．

3. 質問：天気予報をチェックしましたか。

　　答え：＿＿＿＿＿＿＿＿＿＿＿＿＿＿＿＿＿＿＿＿＿＿＿＿＿＿＿＿＿＿＿＿．

4. 質問：宿題は終わりましたか。

　　答え：＿＿＿＿＿＿＿＿＿＿＿＿＿＿＿＿＿＿＿＿＿＿＿＿＿＿＿＿＿＿＿＿．

Which Is Better?

Unit 14

比較級・最上級

Check Points

❶ パーティーのためにどのような料理が用意されているか理解しましょう。
❷ 自分が好きな料理について、比較しながら説明できるようになりましょう。
❸ 比較表現を使った英文に慣れましょう。

Listening Warm Up

A 1〜3のイラストについて英文が読まれます。内容と一致するものはTを、一致しないものはFを○で囲みましょう。

CheckLink　DL 54　CD 54

1.　(T / F)　2.　(T / F)　3.　(T / F)

B ケンジが体重について語っています。1〜3の内容が正しい場合はTを、間違っている場合はFを○で囲みましょう。

CheckLink　DL 55　CD 55

1. Kenji thinks he eats too fast.　(T / F)
2. He weighs five kilos more than he did one year ago.　(T / F)
3. He has started eating healthier food.　(T / F)

77

Conversation

▶ 今日はジャスティンの誕生日です。アキとアリスは食事の用意をしています。

A 会話を聞いて空欄を埋めましょう。　　　DL 56　CD 56

Aki: Alice, the birthday cake you made for Justin is (¹　　　) than the cakes in the cake shops. It's beautiful!

Alice: Thanks, Aki. It took a long time to make, but it was fun.

Aki: What kind of pizza do you think we should get for the party?

Alice: How about two vegetarian pizzas and one with meat?

Aki: Good idea. Which is (²　　　), Pizza King or Premium Pizza?

Alice: Well, I think Premium Pizza makes the (³　　　) (⁴　　　) pizza, and they have the (⁵　　　) (⁶　　　). But it's a little (⁷　　　) (⁸　　　) than Pizza King.

Aki: That's OK. I have a ¥500 yen off coupon for Premium Pizza.

Alice and Aki: Yay!

B もう一度会話を聞いて、1〜3の英文について、適切な語を選びましょう。　CheckLink

1. Alice (**a.** made **b.** didn't have enough time to make) Justin's cake.
2. Aki and Alice are going to get (**a.** two **b.** three) pizzas.
3. They are going to get the pizzas from (**a.** Pizza King **b.** Premium Pizza).

C クラスメートとペアを組んで、アキとアリスの会話を声に出して練習してみましょう。

Grammar Points

Which Is Better? Unit **14**

> **まずはこれを覚えよう!**
>
> Canada is bigger than the United States.
> 「カナダはアメリカよりも大きいです」
> Ken is the smallest boy in the class. 「ケンはクラスで一番小柄です」
> This shop makes the most delicious cake in town.
> 「この店は街で一番おいしいケーキを作ります」

● 比較級・最上級の作り方

	原形（もとの形）	比較級	最上級
-er/-est 系	nice（良い） healthy（健康的な）	nicer healthier	the nicest the healthiest
more/most 系	delicious（おいしい） expensive（高価な）	more delicious more expensive	the most delicious the most expensive
不規則変化	good（良い） bad（悪い）	better worse	the best the worst

● 比較級の基本語順

［主語（誰／何が）］+［動詞（〜する／〜です）］+［比較級 (-er/more-)］+［than］+［比較対象］

主語（誰が）	動詞	比較級 (-er/more-)	than	比較対象	
Canada	is	bigger	than	the United States.	「カナダはアメリカよりも大きいです」
Beef	is	more expensive	than	chicken.	「牛肉は鶏肉より高いです」

● 最上級の基本語順

［主語（誰／何が）］+［動詞（〜する／〜です）］+［the］+［最上級 (-est/most-)］+［範囲］

主語（誰が）	動詞	the	最上級 (-est/most-)	範囲	
Ken	is	the	smallest boy	in the class.	「ケンはクラスで一番小柄です」
This shop	makes	the	most delicious cake	in town.	「この店は街で一番おいしいケーキを作ります」

Grammar Check

A （　）内のa〜cから適当なものを選び、〇で囲みましょう。

1. Today is (a. warm b. warmer c. more warm) than yesterday.
2. Doug has (a. a better b. better a c. better) computer than me.
3. Kim is (a. fastest b. a fastest c. the fastest) runner on the team.
4. Saori is (a. taller b. more tall c. taller than) Natsuki.
5. This is (a. the most interesting b. the interesting c. most interesting) book I have read.
6. Fruit is (a. healthy b. healthier c. more healthier) than candy.
7. Where is the (a. good b. better c. best) place to go shopping in your city?
8. Gold is (a. heavy than silver b. silver heavier than c. heavier than silver).
9. Mount Fuji is (a. the tallest mountain b. tallest the mountain c. the tallest a mountain) in Japan.
10. Tokyo is (a. more modern b. a more modern c. more modern a) city than Kyoto.

B （　）内の語句を並べ替えて文を作りましょう。

1. (are / bigger / chimpanzees / gorillas / than)　「ゴリラはチンパンジーよりも大きいです」
   _____.

2. (is / river / what / longest / the)　「世界で一番長い川は何ですか」
   _____ in the world?

3. (the / hotel / is / expensive / most)　「ウィンザーホテルはその街で一番高いホテルです」
   The Windsor Hotel _____ in the city.

4. (best / the / player / is / who)　「あなたのバレーボール部の中で一番うまい選手は誰ですか」
   _____ on your volleyball team?

Unit 14 Which Is Better?

Express Yourself

A アリスが好きな食べ物について書いています。英文を読んで内容を理解しましょう。

DL 57 CD 57

Two foods that I like are tacos and hamburgers. I think tacos are healthier than hamburgers. They have a lot of fresh vegetables in them. They are also spicier. But hamburgers are more popular than tacos. They are easier to make, and they are cheaper, too.

B 上の英文を参考にして、あなたのお気に入りの食べ物を比較して説明する英文を書いてみましょう。

項目	英文
好きな 食べ物2つ	My favorite foods are (¹) and (²).
どちらがより 好きか	I like (³) better (⁴) (⁵).
どちらがより 健康的か	I think (⁶) (is / are) (⁷) (⁸) (⁹).
どちらがより 簡単に作れるか	(¹⁰) (is / are) (¹¹) to make.
どちらがより 値段が安いか	(¹²) (is / are) (¹³) (¹⁴) (¹⁵).

Hints
- 「…より〜が好き」like 〜 better than… ・「健康的な」healthy
- 「簡単に作れる」easy to make ・「値段が安い」cheap

Unit 15 Surprise!

受動態

Check Points

❶ サプライズ誕生日パーティーでの4人の様子について、情報を理解しましょう。
❷ 自分のお気に入りの本や音楽について、英語で説明できるようになりましょう。
❸ 受動態を使った英文に慣れましょう。

Listening Warm Up

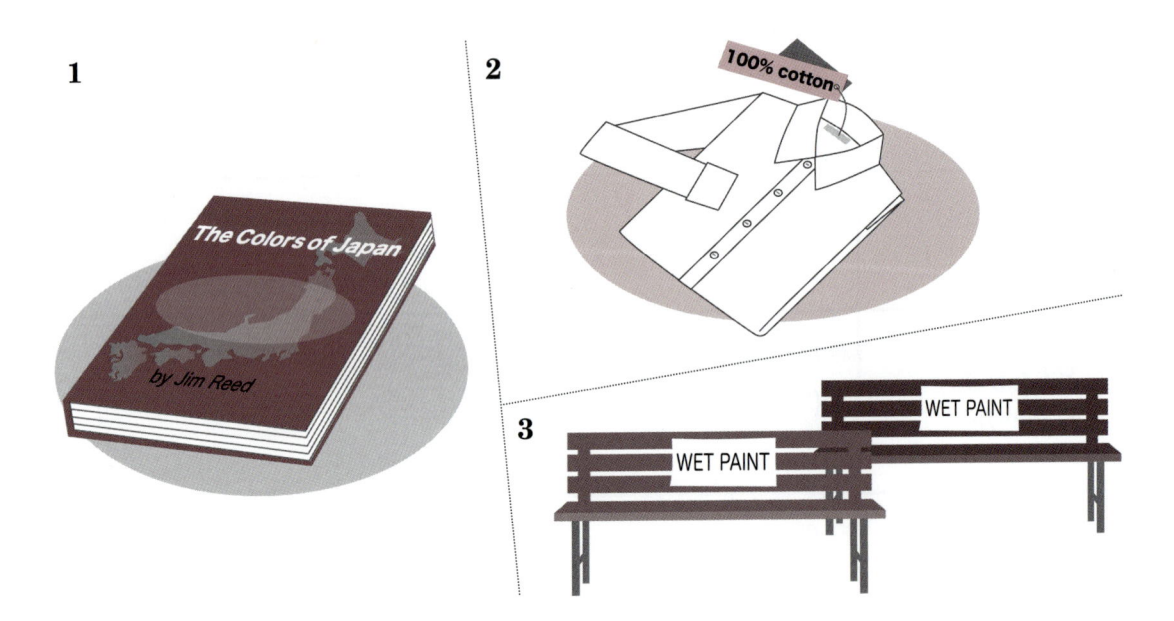

A 1〜3のイラストについて英文が読まれます。内容と一致するものはTを、一致しないものはFを○で囲みましょう。

CheckLink　DL 58　CD 58

1.

2.

3.

1. (T / F)　2. (T / F)　3. (T / F)

B アキがアルバイト先で起こったことを話しています。1〜3の内容が正しい場合はTを、間違っている場合はFを○で囲みましょう。

CheckLink　DL 59　CD 59

1. Aki worked this morning.　(T / F)
2. Aki got sick after work.　(T / F)
3. There will be a surprise birthday party for Justin tonight.　(T / F)

Conversation

▶ ケンジとジャスティンはアキの家に着きました。ジャスティンは驚いてくれるでしょうか。

A 会話を聞いて空欄を埋めましょう。　　DL 60　CD 60

All:　　SURPRISE!!!　Happy Birthday!
Justin:　This *is* a surprise. Wow! Look at that cake. It's beautiful.
Aki:　　The cake (¹　　　) (²　　　　) by Alice.
Alice:　And the message (³　　　) (⁴　　　　　) in Japanese. It says "Happy Birthday Justin."
Justin:　Oh! Let me take a picture before it (⁵　　　) (⁶　　　　).
Kenji:　…And here's a birthday present from all of us. Here, open it.
Justin:　Thanks. Oh, it's a book. …*Sketches of Japan.*
Aki:　　They (⁷　　　) all (⁸　　　　) by famous Japanese artists.
Justin:　It's perfect! Thanks everyone.
Kenji:　You're welcome. …OK, let's have a party!

B もう一度会話を聞いて、1〜3の英文について、適切な語を選びましょう。　CheckLink

1. The message on the birthday cake is in (**a.** English　**b.** Japanese).
2. Justin takes a picture of his birthday cake (**a.** before　**b.** after) it is cut.
3. Justin's birthday present is a book of (**a.** sketches　**b.** photographs) of Japan.

C クラスメートと組んで、4人の会話を声に出して練習してみましょう。

83

Grammar Points

> **まずは これを 覚えよう!**
>
> Swahili is spoken in African countries.
> 「スワヒリ語はアフリカの国々で話されています」
> This picture was taken by a famous photographer.
> 「この写真は有名な写真家によって撮られました」
> This shirt is made of silk. 「このシャツは絹で作られています」

● 受動態の働き

「～される」と、動作を受けることを表現する場合は受動態（受け身形）を使います。

● 基本語順

主語（誰が）	be動詞	過去分詞	その他の情報	
Apples	are	grown	in Aomori Prefecture.	「リンゴは青森県で育てられています」

● 様々な受動態の表現

受動態の動作が誰によって行われたかを表現するときはbyを使います。
These cookies were made by my mother. 「これらのクッキーは私の母によって作られました」
商品などの原材料を表現するときにも受動態を使います。
This ring is made of gold. 「この指輪は金で作られています」
This ice cream is made from soy beans. 「このアイスは大豆から作られています」

● その他の表現

Peter was told not to leave the room. 「ピーターはその部屋を出ないように言われた」

● 否定文と疑問文

否定文を作るときはbe動詞の後ろにnotをつけます。
疑問文を作るときは主語とbe動詞の順番を入れ替えます。

	This book is read by children.	「この本は子どもたちに読まれています」
否定文	This book isn't read by children.	「この本は子どもたちに読まれていません」
疑問文	Is this book read by children?	「この本は子どもたちに読まれていますか」

Grammar Check

A ( )内のa～cから適当なものを選び、◯で囲みましょう。

1. Alice (a. born b. is born c. was born) in Seattle.
2. The carpet (a. is clean b. is cleaned c. is cleaning) once a week.
3. The news (a. was hear b. was heard c. were hear) around the world.
4. These sketches (a. made b. was made c. were made) by Aki.
5. The students (a. were tell b. was told c. were told) not to talk in the library.
6. Spanish (a. is spoken b. is speak c. is spoke) in Peru.
7. What sports (a. are played b. is played c. are playing) in Thailand?
8. The letter (a. was wrote b. was written c. were written) by Janet.
9. These cars (a. selling b. sold c. are sold) only in Japan.
10. The money (a. found b. was found c. was founded) in a forest.

B ( )内の語句を並べ替えて文を作りましょう。

1. (played / many / countries / in / is) 「サッカーはたくさんの国で競技されています」
   Soccer _____.

2. (cotton / *yukata* / of / is / made) 「この浴衣は綿で作られています」
   This _____.

3. (anyone / the accident / in / was / hurt) 「誰かその事故でけがをしましたか」
   _____?

4. (not / very / room / used / is) 「この部屋はそれほど頻繁には使われていません」
   This _____ often.

5. (these / taken / pictures / were / where) 「これらの写真はどこで撮られたのですか」
   _____?

85

Express Yourself

A ジャスティンが好きな本、歌、絵画を紹介しています。英文を読んで内容を理解しましょう。

DL 61　CD 61

Let me tell you about some of my favorite works. My favorite book is *The Old Man and the Sea*. It was written by Ernest Hemingway. My favorite song is "I Don't Want to Miss a Thing." It is sung by Aerosmith. My favorite painting is *Water Lilies*. It was painted by Claude Monet.

B 上の英文を参考にして、あなたの好きな本や漫画、歌、絵画、映画について英語で書いてみましょう。

項目	英文
好きな本／漫画	My favorite (¹　　　　) is (²　　　　　　).
作者	It was (³　　　　) by (⁴　　　　　　).
好きな歌	My favorite (⁵　　　　) is (⁶　　　　　　).
歌手	It is (⁷　　　　) by (⁸　　　　　　).
好きな絵画	My favorite (⁹　　　　) is (¹⁰　　　　　　).
作者	It was (¹¹　　　　) by (¹²　　　　　　).
好きな映画	My favorite movie is (¹³　　　　　　).
主演	The leading role was (¹⁴　　　　) by (¹⁵　　　　　　).

Hints　●「(本や漫画を)書く／描く」write　●「(役割を)演じる」play

付録

▶「基本例文」一覧

Unit 1 [be 動詞]	
☐ 私は18歳です。	I am 18 years old.
☐ あなたはおとなしい人です。	You are a quiet person.
☐ ジャスティンは恥ずかしがり屋です。	Justin is shy.

Unit 2 [一般動詞]	
☐ ジャスティンはカメラが大好きです。	Justin likes cameras very much.
☐ 授業には辞書を持ってきなさい。	Bring your dictionary to class.
☐ 私は今日は特に予定はありません。	I don't have any plans today.

Unit 3 [代名詞]	
☐ これは私の兄です。彼の名前はジョンです。	This is my brother. His name is John.
☐ ジョンソンさんなら知っています。私は彼女と昨日会いました。	I know Mrs. Johnson. I met her yesterday.
☐ 私の母はパンを焼きます。それは美味しいです。	My mother bakes bread. It is delicious.

Unit 4 [場所を表す前置詞]	
☐ 私のリュックサックの中には何も入っていません。	There's nothing in my backpack.
☐ 私は帽子とサングラスをリュックサックの上に置きました。	I put a hat and sunglasses on the backpack.
☐ あなたの靴はテーブルの下です。	Your shoes are under the table.

Unit 5 [Yes・Noで答える疑問文]	
☐ ジュリエットはハワイ出身ですか。	Is Juliet from Hawaii?
☐ あなたはスペイン語を話しますか。	Do you speak Spanish?
☐ あなたのお兄さんはバイオリンを弾きますか。	Does your brother play the violin?

Unit 6 [現在進行形・過去進行形]		
☐	私は今、朝食を作っています。	I am making breakfast now.
☐	ケンはその時、友達とバスケットボールをしていました。	Ken was playing basketball with his friends then.
☐	あなたのお姉さんは今ステージで歌っていません。	Your sister is not singing on stage now.
Unit 7 [一般動詞の過去形]		
☐	私は昨日剣道の練習をしました。	I practiced *kendo* yesterday.
☐	アリスは数学のテスト勉強をしなかった。	Alice didn't study for the math test.
☐	リサとボブは良いアパートを見つけましたか。	Did Lisa and Bob find a nice apartment?
Unit 8 [助動詞]		
☐	私は日本語と英語が話せます。	I can speak Japanese and English.
☐	私はこの本をマイに渡さなければならない。	I must give this book to Mai.
☐	私はお昼ご飯を持っていくべきですか。	Should I bring my lunch with me?
Unit 9 [疑問詞]		
☐	あなたはポケットの中に何を持っていますか。	What do you have in your pocket?
☐	あなたはどこへ行きたいのですか。	Where do you want to go?
☐	あなたはこれを英語でどう言いますか。	How do you say this in English?
Unit 10 [不定詞・動名詞]		
☐	今夜このレポートを仕上げる必要があります。	You need to finish this report tonight.
☐	バトラーさんは日本で英語を教えることを楽しんでいます。	Ms. Butler enjoys teaching English in Japan.
☐	アリスは毎日漢字を書く練習をします。	Alice practices writing *kanji* every day.

	Unit 11 [未来形]	
☐	私はスマートフォンを買う予定です。	I'm going to buy a smartphone.
☐	あなたのスーツケースを持ってあげましょう。	I will carry your suitcase.
☐	監督は今日、試合に来ません。	Our coach won't come to the game today.
	Unit 12 [接続詞]	
☐	ジョンは土曜日に働き、そして日曜日にゴルフをします。	John works on Saturdays and plays golf on Sundays.
☐	テッドは頭はいいけれど怠け者です。	Ted is smart but lazy.
☐	外食しますか、それとも家で食べたいですか。	Shall we go out for dinner, or do you want to eat at home?
	Unit 13 [現在完了形]	
☐	私はオーストラリアに行ったことがあります。	I have been to Australia.
☐	ずいぶん長いこと彼女には会っていません。	I haven't seen her for a long time.
☐	宿題をやり終えましたか。	Have you finished your homework?
	Unit 14 [比較級・最上級]	
☐	カナダはアメリカよりも大きいです。	Canada is bigger than the United States.
☐	ケンはクラスで一番小柄です。	Ken is the smallest boy in the class.
☐	この店は街で一番おいしいケーキを作ります。	This shop makes the most delicious cake in town.
	Unit 15 [受動態]	
☐	スワヒリ語はアフリカの国々で話されています。	Swahili is spoken in African countries.
☐	この写真は有名な写真家によって撮られました。	This picture was taken by a famous photographer.
☐	このシャツは絹で作られています。	This shirt is made of silk.

▶「不規則変化動詞」一覧

現在形	過去形	過去分詞形
be「〜である」	was/were	been
bring「持っていく」	brought	brought
buy「買う」	bought	bought
catch「捕まえる」	caught	caught
come「来る」	came	come
choose「選ぶ」	chose	chosen
do「する」	did	done
draw「描く」	drew	drawn
eat「食べる」	ate	eaten
find「見つける」	found	found
forget「忘れる」	forgot	forgot/forgotten
get「得る」	got	got/gotten
give「与える」	gave	given
go「行く」	went	gone
have「持つ」	had	had
hear「聞く」	heard	heard
hit「打つ」	hit	hit
know「知る」	knew	known
leave「去る」	left	left
lose「失う」	lost	lost
make「作る」	made	made
put「置く」	put	put
read「読む」	read	read
say「言う」	said	said
see「見る」	saw	seen
sell「売る」	sold	sold
sing「歌う」	sang	sung
take「取る」	took	taken
tell「話す」	told	told
think「考える」	thought	thought
write「書く」	wrote	written